Plants, beds and borders

Katie Rushworth

KYLE BOOKS

Plants, beds and borders

Create and maintain your perfect garden

Katie Rushworth

Photography by Paul Debois

KYLE BOOKS

To Polly: dream big, persevere and be as kind to yourself as you are to others in the process.

You can achieve anything.

First published in Great Britain in 2016 by
Kyle Books, an imprint of Kyle Cathie Ltd
192–198 Vauxhall Bridge Road
London SW1V 1DX
general.enquiries@kylebooks.com
www.kylebooks.co.uk

10 9 8 7 6 5 4 3 2 1

ISBN 978 0 85783 285 6

The images on the following pages were taken at Dove Cottage in Yorkshire with the kind permission of the owners: 9, 13 top left, 27, 28, 32 bottom, 40 bottom right, 40 bottom left, 55 right, 56 top, 58, 59 bottom, 60, 73 left, 81 bottom right, 88 bottom right, 98 top, 101 right and far right, 102 top, 111 bottom left, 111 right, 112 bottom, 115 bottom, 117, 118, 120 bottom, 122 bottom, 123 left, 129 left, 136 left, 139, 170 left, 171 left, middle and right.

Project Editor: Tara O'Sullivan
Editorial Assistant: Amberley Lowis
Copy Editor: Polly Boyd
Designer: Dale Walker
Photographer: Paul Debois
Illustrator: Sarah Beeston
Production: Lisa Pinnell

A Cataloguing in Publication record for this title is available from the British Library.

Colour reproduction by ALTA London
Printed and bound in China by C&C Offset Printing Co., Ltd

Contents

Introduction

Gardens are becoming more and more important in our fast-paced, technology-driven lives – they offer a peaceful sanctuary from modern life and give us the chance to get close to the natural world. There is something soothing and relaxing about being surrounded by nature and feeling part of a bigger picture. Most people can relate to and enjoy this emotional connection; for some it can be buried deep, but I believe it's something that is in us all – it just needs a gentle nudge. Whether you want to use your garden to sit with a glass of wine and unwind after a day at work, or as somewhere to entertain friends or play games with your children, it's well worth investing some time and money to transform it into a wonderful place to be.

Since starting work as a garden designer I have found the same conversation always comes up, whether I'm meeting with a client or chatting to friends down at the pub. People tell me they know what they want – a beautiful garden that reflects their lifestyle and personality – but they don't know how to achieve it. Often they have a limited budget or need to be able to attain the look they want without completely re-landscaping their garden. And the secret to totally transforming your outside space is simple: it's all about the borders.

Most of us are accustomed to considering and designing the interior of our homes to make the most of the space we have and to reflect tastes and style. The size of some gardens can be equal to, or even bigger than, the floor plan of the property, so it makes sense to make the most of them. You can maximise this potential with striking planting, colourfully planted pots, architectural foliage and some choice specimen plants.

I hope that this book will take away the fear from the idea of transforming your garden, whether you're developing an existing space or starting from scratch with a blank canvas. Like most projects, designing is a process that requires a series of stages – gathering information, drawing

'Transform your garden into a wonderful place to be'

Dove Cottage

up lists of requirements and so on – and once you've established the foundations you can build on these with confidence.

In the chapters that follow, we will explore the ways in which borders can revitalise and reinvent your garden. Gardens, like people, come in all shapes and sizes – some are well manicured and look young; others have great maturity and may need a little TLC to look their best! I will guide you through the process of creating beautiful borders that will provide interest in the garden throughout the year. I'll break down the basic principles of garden design, giving you top tips on how to unify your space – no matter how large or small – and pointers on how to pull a garden together using colour, shape and texture. When these design principles are applied in combination with each other they will really make your borders sing.

And of course I have included plenty of information about the plants themselves – how you can achieve successful planting schemes and create particular garden styles, such as a cottage garden, formal garden, wildlife garden or family garden. I give plenty of examples of how to use plants to create different moods and atmospheres and recommend top varieties to grow for maximum perfume that will seduce the senses and give your garden that extra 'wow' factor. A practical section advises on how to plant and look after your new borders and provides insider knowledge on how to make borders chock-full of plants on the cheap. Finally, we'll look beyond the borders to extra features and ideas to give your garden additional sparkle.

It is worth being absolutely clear from the beginning that gardening is not about instant satisfaction – you must be patient. Accepting that now before you get going is probably the best advice I can give you. Also, it's important to remember that gardens evolve constantly; they develop over the years and have huge seasonal shifts of interest and growth, so try to plan ahead to anticipate these changes. The research and time you put in to designing now are sure to pay dividends in the future, resulting in a garden that will improve with age and grow old gracefully.

Chapter 1
Planning your borders

Revamping your garden by designing new borders is an exciting prospect. However, it can seem like a huge undertaking – especially for the novice gardener. The key to success is to plan carefully from the beginning; a little thought and time invested at the start will pay off later.

When and how to plan

Winter is a great time to start planning a new garden – and not just because you can do it from the comfort of the sofa! Once plants die back and the ground is exposed, your garden really shows its bare bones, so you can see the basic framework and structure.

Also, while the weather is colder and there are fewer maintenance tasks to carry out in the garden, take the opportunity to research and plan from the comfort of your home – look through books and magazines and browse the internet for inspiration.

Take your time

It's important to take your time at the planning stage. This approach is taken by all professional garden designers and will give you a far better design that will mature well over the years.

If you're moving into a new property, give yourself at least a year to become acquainted with the garden before making any changes. Bulbs may come up you didn't know were there, herbaceous perennials like Michaelmas daisies (*Aster amellus*) will not show their brilliance until September, boggy ground may become apparent after a heavy downpour, and the winter sun might only manage to cast its rays over half of what is your sunniest border in the summer. All these variables are invaluable nuggets of knowledge when considering any new garden project.

Even if you are simply revamping your current garden, it's still worth taking notes throughout the year – record which plants have done well and which never thrive, what you definitely want to keep and what you would like more of. Take photographs and make notes as, once plants stop flowering and are past their best, it can be difficult to recall why you liked something and what it looked like. You also see a garden very differently in a photograph and become more aware of the different shapes of plants, the different levels in their heights, and how they work together to provide interest within the space.

It is a good idea to retain some established trees and shrubs in your new design – they will give even the most basic

Dove Cottage

and uninspiring garden a sense of maturity. If you don't plan on staying in the house for long, try your best to work with what you already have – what looks like a tired shrub or old rose can sometimes come back great guns if pruned correctly and given a good feed.

Making your plan of action

Whether you're creating an entirely new garden, designing a new border or replanting certain areas that are lacklustre or not flourishing, drawing up a planting plan before you start is a great way to tackle any area of your garden – put pen to paper before you reach for the spade, and use your brain before your brawn.

First, really get to know your garden and compile a list of site conditions. Next, identify what you want from your garden based on your lifestyle, style preferences and time you can realistically spend on maintenance (see page 22). Do your research on plants and choose varieties that will suit the conditions in your garden as well as your chosen garden style (see pages 68–139); there is no point in planting something you love but which won't thrive.

Armed with all this knowledge, draw a very simple plan of your garden (see page 38). The benefit of a plan is it will give you a clear vision of what space you are working with and you can experiment with new layouts and planting schemes without committing until you are fully clued up on what will work and what won't. Any mistakes will be made on paper first, saving you time, money, hard labour and the frustration of getting it wrong in reality.

▲ **A great example of a well-planned border.**
▼ **Michaelmas daisies come into their own in September.**

◄ **Taking the time to plan your garden will make everything easier in the long run.**

Working with **what you have**

Before you start planning your new garden or borders, you need to think about the practicalities. To grow healthy plants you need to understand the existing garden's features, such as its aspect, orientation and layout, and the quality of the soil and its capacity for drainage. All gardens have pros and cons, but knowing them and using them to your advantage will give you a real sense of satisfaction when you see the results.

Size and shape

Gardens come in an enormous variety of shapes and sizes. Re-designing a large garden can seem like an unachievable task to the novice, and a small garden can be frustrating when it comes to trying to accommodate all your requirements. This is where zoning comes in. Dividing a garden into sections will allow you to create zones that will each have their specific aspect, orientation and layout. Tackling zones one at a time in a large garden will break up the project into bite-sized chunks. In a small garden, try giving your zones more than one job: the shady part of your garden would be ideal for woodland plants, and also a children's play area, while the south-facing part of your plot could have raised vegetable beds that double up as seating. A little imagination is needed and planning is essential.

Setting

Another thing to consider when designing your garden is the location. Do you live in a rural environment or have a city apartment? The best gardens are those that sit comfortably in their surroundings, and incorporating plants and materials that are already an existing part of the garden's locality will result in a garden that blends into its setting.

If you have a garden with a wonderful view, then it is worth considering how to frame it and link it to the garden, creating a seamless transition outwards and into the landscape beyond. This is called a 'borrowed landscape', and it's a particularly popular technique in naturalistic gardens (see pages 106–115). Using plants and materials in a way that echoes your view will create a connection between your garden and its surroundings.

Aspect and orientation

Note how the sun travels across your garden at different times of the day, ideally in both summer and winter. Where the sun reaches and doesn't reach will dramatically affect both the soil and the plants you want to grow there – for instance, an area that gets no sun in winter may be heavy and wet, particularly if it's a clay soil; a border that gets sun all day can be extremely dry in summer, especially if the soil is sandy. These are areas that will certainly need the right kind of plants to cope with the difficulty of the conditions (see page 18).

Look out of the window

You want your view to be pretty all year, so look out of the windows when you're planning your garden to make sure you give yourself a great view. Be sure to look from the upstairs windows too – this is a great vantage point when considering your border options. This bird's eye view will make it easier to see how your existing paths and new borders will link together.

◀ Using materials local to the area, such as this drystone walling, links the garden to its surroundings.

Soil type

The type of soil you have in your garden plays a major role in working out what plants you can grow successfully. It can also dictate the style and theme most suitable for your garden. Soil can vary in texture, consistency and how it works with water. Most plants prefer deep, well-drained, fertile soil, but there are many that can survive in challenging situations – so find out what you're working with and choose your plants accordingly. You can improve the soil by adding plenty of organic matter at the time of planting or by mulching around existing plants (see pages 146–147). Digging, watering and feeding (see pages 142 and 145–146) will also help.

▶ *Thalictrums* are well suited to clay soil.

▼ *Eryngiums* thrive in sandy soil.

How to work out your soil type

The bucket test is a quick and easy way to work out what kind of soil you have. Take a bucket of water and a handful of soil from your garden, ideally from at least 25cm below ground level. Dunk your hand into the bucket for a few seconds, keeping hold of the soil. Now take your hand out of the bucket and look at the soil. If it sticks together and clumps, it's clay based. If it stays loose and won't stick together, it's free draining. Easy.

Clay soil

Also called heavy soil, clay soil is made up of many small particles that stick together, making it hard for water to drain. It easily compacts when wet and can set hard like concrete in a dry summer, making it tough to dig. It takes a long time to warm up in the spring. On the plus side, it is fairly fertile and lots of lush foliage plants thrive in it. Adding organic matter (see page 142) will improve the texture of clay soil greatly over time.

▲ Choose plants that thrive in your type of soil.

Silt soil

This is a combination of clay and sandy soils in terms of texture and consistency. It drains fairly well, yet holds on to more water than a sandy soil. It is usually high in nutrients too, but can become compacted quickly due to its fine particles. Again, adding organic matter will bind the particles to a more stable crumb.

Loam

Loam is a mixture of clay, sandy and silt soils. It is the easiest soil to work with and is fertile, well drained and easy to dig. Because this soil rarely becomes water-logged or dried out, it can support a huge array of plants. However, you will still need to add organic matter regularly to keep that 'perfect' balance.

Sandy soil

Sandy or 'light' soil is far easier to dig than clay. It is free draining and warms up quickly in spring. However, it is less fertile and very quick to dry out in summer. You can beef up your sandy soil by adding lots of organic matter, which will help it to hold on to moisture and nutrients. Many Mediterranean plants love it.

Chalky soil

Chalky soil can be light or quite heavy, often with visible lumps of chalk and white stone. It is invariably alkaline (see Soil pH, page 19) and often shallow and free draining, so choose your plants carefully.

◀ *Geranium pratense* grows well in chalky soil.

Wet soil

Soil that is continually wet is very limiting in terms of what will grow. However, there are many magnificent plants that thrive in these conditions, particularly tropical-looking architectural plants with large leaves and brightly coloured flowers – for instance *Ligularia*, *Rodgersia* and bamboos. A good mulch of organic matter every spring will improve the condition of the soil.

Plants by soil type

This table shows you which plants thrive in different types of soil. Some plants are mentioned in two soil types – this is because many plants will tolerate a variety of soils, especially if competition from weeds is kept down, and the garden is mulched once a year. I haven't provided a plant list for loam soil as it can support such a huge array of plants – just pick your favourites!

Clay soil	Chalky soil	Sandy soil	Silt soil	Wet soil
Aruncus	*Agapanthus*	*Acer palmatum*	*Aconitum*	*Actaea*
Astilbe	*Buxus*	*Achillea*	*Calamagrostis*	*Astilbe*
Astrantia	*Ceanothus*	*Agastache*	*Camellia*	*Cornus*
Buxus	*Chionodoxa*	*Amelanchier*	*Deschampsia*	*Darmera peltata*
Calamagrostis	*Clematis*	*Cistus*	*Digitalis*	*Filipendula*
Cornus	*Cotinus coggygria*	*Crambe cordifolia*	*Hakonechloa*	*Gunnera manicata*
Euonymus	*Cotoneaster*	*Crataegus laevigata*	*Hyacinthoides*	*Hosta*
Eupatorium	*Crataegus*	*Dianthus*	*Laburnum*	*Hydrangea paniculata*
Fatsia	*Crocosmia*	*carthusianorum*	*Mahonia*	*Iris pseudacorus*
Geum	*Dianthus*	*Echinacea*	*Malus sylvestris*	*Iris sibirica*
Hosta	*Dicentra*	*Erigeron*	*Paeonia*	*Ligularia*
Humulus	*Echinacea pallida*	*karvinskianus*	*Phormium*	*Liquidambar*
Hydrangea	*Erysimum*	*Eryngium*	*Pyracantha*	*styraciflua*
Lythrum	*Euonymus fortunei*	*Kniphofia*	*Rodgersia*	*Lobelia cardinalis*
Mahonia × media	*Fagus sylvatica*	*Lavandula*	*Rudbeckia*	*Lysichiton americanus*
Monarda	*Geranium*	*Nepeta*	*Vitis*	*Lythrum*
Nandina domestica	*Hebe*	*Perovskia*		*Matteuccia*
Osmanthus ×	*Lavandula*	*Phlomis fruticosa*		*struthiopteris*
burkwoodii	*Lonicera nitida*	*Salvia*		*Phyllostachys*
Persicaria	*Miscanthus nepalensis*	*Santolina*		*Primula florindae*
Phlox paniculata	*Persicaria affinis*	*Sedum*		*Primula japonica*
Polemonium	*Potentilla*	*Sorbus*		*Rheum palmatum*
Primula	*Stipa*	*Stachys byzantina*		*Rodgersia pinnata*
Roses (Rosa)	*Verbascum*	*Stipa*		*Salix*
Sambucus		*Verbascum*		*Zantedeschia*
Sarcococca				*aethiopica*
Syringa				
Taxus baccata				
Thalictrum				

Soil pH

It is useful to know your soil pH (acid-alkaline balance) when choosing plants, so you know what will thrive or not. You can do a simple pH test using an inexpensive kit from the garden centre: pH1 is very acidic, ph7 is neutral and pH14 is very alkaline. Most soils are somewhere in the middle of the range, which is ideal for most plants. However, some plants, such as rhododendrons, camellias and azaleas, require acid conditions (pH6 and below) and will not thrive in soil pH7 and above (alkaline soils). Other plants, such as *Ceanothus*, *Cotinus* and *Osmanthus*, prefer alkaline conditions.

You can add lime to acid soils to increase the number of plants you can grow there, but there is little you can do to make alkaline soil more acidic, so choose suitable plants and regularly add organic matter.

◀ *Iris sibirica* will thrive in wet soil.

Take a look around

Look into your neighbours' gardens – what is growing well for them that you like the look of? If it grows well for them, it is more than likely it will also grow well for you, as your gardens probably share similar conditions.

Slopes

Slopes can be difficult to work with, especially if they are steep. However, there are things you can do – it just takes a little more planning, as well as extra labour and expense.

Terraces

The first option I tend to consider in a sloping garden is creating terraces. These not only lead you down the slope gradually, but also give you more levels to plant, meaning you can fit more in!

Banks

Another way of treating slopes is to create banks. However, these can be difficult to plant and maintain and, unless you're a mountain goat, weeding a banked area is hard going. In these situations I always plant low-maintenance ground cover that will help knit together the soil and make a weed-suppressing thicket. My favourites are carpet roses – I have had real success using a Flower Carpet rose on a steep bank and it just gets more magnificent every year; the simple flowers are not only attractive but a great source of food for the birds. Other plants that are good for banks are *Cotoneaster*, periwinkle (*Vinca*), heaths (*Erica*), *Geranium*, juniper (*Juniperus horizontalis*), *Pachysandra*, *Persicaria bistorta* 'Superba' and *Stachys byzantina*.

Wind protection

If your garden is prone to wind turbulence, hard prune any shrubs with long top-growth, such as buddleia (*Buddleja*) and roses (*Rosa*), in autumn to prevent wind rock (see Pruning, pages 154–155).

Climate and microclimates

Although general conditions in the garden are determined by the local climate and weather, every garden has its own microclimates – spots that are windier, colder, drier or wetter. It's important to get to know your garden well so you can identify the microclimates and choose plants that will thrive in these often challenging sites.

Wind and wind tunnels

I have designed many exposed gardens and have seen the devastation that wind can have on newly planted trees and shrubs. Wind rock can occur, which is when the wind shakes the top-growth of a plant so much that the roots are disturbed and the plant is weakened. In some extreme cases, the wind can actually uproot whole shrubs and even trees.

The best approach to dealing with wind turbulence is to plant hedging, which will filter the wind and slow it in its path. Some properties have a boundary of hedges planted for this very reason; this is known as a shelterbelt.

If you plant trees in an area with wind turbulence, you must ensure that they are adequately staked and well secured with a tree tie.

Sometimes wind is funnelled through narrow spaces, making it even stronger and more damaging, particularly if it squeezes through solid structures such as between buildings and walls. You will need to plant very tough plants for these spaces, and/or create a barrier in the form of a windbreak such as a fence or hedge.

Below is a list of plants that are suitable for this use:

- *Acer pseudoplatanus* (sycamore)
- *Berberis*
- *Crataegus monogyna* (hawthorn) – hedge
- *Elaeagnus* – hedge
- *Erica*
- *Geranium*
- *Griselinia littoralis* – hedge
- *Hebe*
- *Helianthemum*
- *Ilex* (holly) – hedge
- *Molinia caerulea*
- *Philadelphus*
- *Pinus sylvestris* L. (Scots pine) – hedge
- *Rosa rugosa* – hedge
- *Salix* (willow) – hedge
- *Taxus baccata* (yew) – hedge
- *Ulex europaeus*

Frost pockets

Cold air can collect in certain areas of the garden, resulting in 'frost pockets'. These areas are slower to warm up after icy weather and quicker to cool down at night. A north-facing wall in winter will most likely get no sun at its base so the soil beneath is constantly in the shade and never warms up (assuming you are in the northern hemisphere). If your garden is on a slope it will always be colder at the bottom than at the top, as cold air rolls and falls down hills.

Make sure that only your reliably hardy plants are grown in frost pockets and keep an eye on your plants over winter. You could consider covering plants with horticultural fleece when you have an extreme cold spell (see page 155).

A simple mistake many people make is to plant spring-flowering trees, shrubs and bulbs in frost pockets. Frost will damage all early blossom, so play it safe and plant these early bloomers in a more temperate part of the garden.

Flooding and waterlogging

If an area of your garden floods regularly it might be worth considering installing some land drains. These are perforated pipes that are laid underground – excess water seeps into them and they drain it away to a designated site that can cope with the overflow. It can be costly, but in the long term may be the best option.

You can also tackle waterlogging by creating raised beds or level changes in a garden. Raising the levels of problem areas and installing good drainage underneath is a big job, but worth the investment. Another option is creating a swale – this looks like a planted up dry river bed, but is transformed into a stream after a good downpour.

▲ If your land is damp, choosing plants that will thrive in this environment, such as this bright orange *Geum*, will help your garden look its best.

Underground services

When undertaking work in the garden it is vital to establish the location and depth of any pipework and cables for services like water, sewage, gas, electricity and phone lines. Cables should be avoided at all costs when digging below ground, as the consequences of any damage can be serious and costly. You may need to contact the relevant utility companies to find out the location of underground services.

Working out
what you really want

▲ Low maintenance plants, like this Acer and Hosta, are good for small spaces.
► If you have young children, consider including a lawn for playing and robust plants that can stand up to the odd football.

Once you've assessed your garden it's time to think about what you want from your new space. Consider your lifestyle and draw up a wish list of everything you'd like your garden to offer.

Be realistic

All gardens require maintenance, so if you want a garden to look good all year round you will need to do some work. However, some gardens are more demanding than others – for instance, a lawn and topiary need regular attention to look their best, and annuals need replacing each year.

It's important that you consider how much time and inclination you have to tend plants – how many hours can you or do you wish to commit to on a weekly basis? A novice gardener who puts in lots of plants that require plenty of maintenance will soon feel like they are out of their depth, and it becomes a disheartening chore to keep up with everything. Be honest with yourself when it comes to the time you can dedicate to maintenance. This will give you a garden that you will enjoy looking after.

Create a wish list

Creating a wish list is a great way to work out an action plan of how to get exactly what you want from your garden. Whether you have the time and money to transform your garden in one go or are more likely to see it as a long-term project, knowing which direction you are going in is the first step. Every wish list will be unique, but to give you an idea of the sorts of things you may want to consider, here are some examples of typical wish lists that I've come across in my work as a garden designer. You might not fit into any of the categories below, but they should give you an idea of the things to consider.

Young professionals
As a young professional couple you might want to entertain friends in an environment that will have its main areas of interest in the summer months. You will probably not have a lot of time for upkeep, so the garden will need to contain mainly easy-care plants – and I'm sure you would love a modern twist in the planting design. Linking a colour from your home to your plants can be the perfect approach. Your wish list might look a little like this:
⊛ No lawn
⊛ Privacy from neighbours (see page 166)
⊛ Low-maintenance plants
⊛ Strong structural planting, mostly evergreen with a pop of colour threading throughout for the summer months
⊛ Screening for shed
⊛ Window boxes for herbs
⊛ Colourful pots with modern planting combinations
⊛ Scent

Family with young children
Family gardens need to please various people of different ages. Creating an outdoor play area for children is a great way to encourage them to engage with nature and drag them away from their tablets and computer games. Ideally, the garden can easily be adapted as the children grow up.

You will probably want a lawn, but bear in mind a natural lawn can be quite high maintenance so you might want to consider an artificial lawn instead (see page 164). You might love the idea of lots of flowers but feel concerned that plants will be damaged by flying footballs and wandering little feet. However, there are many plants that will stand up to a kick about. Here's an example of how your wish list might look:
⊛ Safe play area
⊛ Place to sit and eat as a family
⊛ Quiet spot full of scent where parents can relax
⊛ Hard-wearing lawn
⊛ Storage or screening for children's toys and bikes
⊛ Teenage den
⊛ Tough plants that will cope with a football
⊛ Low-maintenance plants, mostly summer interest
⊛ Vegetable-growing area
⊛ A small plot for the kids to have a go at growing flower seeds and vegetables

Retired couple

If you're retired, you might have extra time to spend in your garden, so borders with year-round interest are a must. You may want to encourage lots of wildlife into your garden and include somewhere to grow vegetables or flowers for cutting. So perhaps your wish list looks like this:

❀ Re-development of borders that have lost their way over the years
❀ Seating areas at different points in the garden to catch the sun at different times of the day
❀ Vegetable beds
❀ Greenhouse for plant propagation
❀ Cutting garden
❀ Lawn
❀ Specimen plants especially for winter interest
❀ Lots of nectar-rich flowers with good seedheads for wildlife

City dwellers

If you live in an urban area, chances are your garden is pretty small – perhaps you only have a tiny backyard or even a balcony. You want to make the most of the space you have, and probably want plants that are tough and will stand up to a higher level of pollutants. Perhaps you'd also like to find plants that can help with soundproofing. In a small space it's particularly important to find plants that will work well all year round, so that you always have something nice to look out on. Your wish list might look like this:

❀ Low maintenance
❀ Evergreen plants
❀ Screening from neighbours
❀ Window boxes with herbs
❀ Bike and/or bin storage
❀ Scented climbers, for walls and fences
❀ A seating area

▲ Your wish list might include a seating area full of scent so that you can enjoy the plants at your leisure.

Finding your personal style

One of the most exciting aspects of designing a garden is making it personal to you, yet it can be difficult to know where to start. Whenever I meet a new client, the first thing I ask them to do is look through magazines and newspapers and cut out pictures of gardens they like, or start a Pinterest board if they enjoy using the internet. I also ask them to collect all manner of things that they like the look, smell or feel of. It's amazing how an object that seems to have nothing to do with gardening can spark an idea – it might be a pebble found on a beach, the pattern on a favourite dress, a sculpture or painting.

All these things can inform you of your design tastes and styles, and once you have collected them together and laid them out on a table you will probably see a common thread of inspiration. It might be a colour palette that crops up regularly, or a certain shape that you are drawn to. By incorporating elements of these into your garden you will instantly make it unique to you and reflect your personal tastes.

The fundamentals
of planting design

Whatever style of garden you're hoping to create, it helps to apply certain fundamental principles used by all garden designers to achieve a cohesive design. These tried-and-tested principles relate to proportion, scale, volume, balance, simplicity, unity and harmony. Consider these the building blocks of your design – it is your personal taste and style that will make your garden unique to you and give your space that *je ne sais quoi*.

▼ Use evergreen plants to give year-round structure, volume and proportion.

Proportion, scale and volume

Think about the size of the garden and make sure the elements within it are in proportion with the space and other features – for example, a pergola of 2 x 2m in a garden measuring 5 x 5m is going to look out of proportion. Consider also the proportions of the house: making sure the heights and widths of features bear some relation to the property will give you a well-proportioned design.

Most gardens I see on first appointments with clients have a lawn in the middle of the plot with slim borders around each side. Proportionally, this looks unbalanced. Designers often use the term 'mass and void' when they are trying to achieve a space that feels balanced. Simply put, 'mass' (or 'stuff', so things like plants, trees, shrubs, outdoor buildings, garden furniture, etc.) needs to be proportionate to the 'void' (or 'space', meaning your paths, patios, lawns and water). I think that one third mass and two thirds void gives a well-proportioned space. However, you can play around with mass and void to find the ratio that works best for you. More mass will make a garden feel enclosed, whereas more void or space will open the garden up and allow access to views out of the garden.

Bear in mind the size of plants, too: a garden containing predominantly large-scale architectural plants may seem oppressive, while a garden full of airy, delicate foliage will seem to lack substance and structure.

Considering volume in your planting design will give you a far richer border. Some plants, such as *Nepeta* 'Six Hills Giant', can grow bushy and dense during the summer months, whereas bronze fennel (*Foeniculum vulgare* 'Purpureum') is tall and graceful. A border containing a variety of plants of different volumes and scales can create a dramatic look.

Balance

It's important to avoid creating a lopsided effect – the feeling that one side of the garden is more dominant than the other. Try to mirror the heights of different plants on either side of the garden so you don't have one side where plants are much higher than the other. Similarly, use

▲ Using a variety of different-sized plants adds scale and depth.

▲ I love the way this planting scheme at Dove Cottage in Yorkshire repeats colour and form to create a feeling of harmony.

Simplicity, unity and harmony

KISS stands for 'Keep It Simple, Stupid', and the saying was always bandied around in my degree course when we got carried away with our designs.

Simple designs are stronger and make a greater impact than fussy schemes. Using a basic framework of structural shrubs and a limited colour palette will give a pleasing effect, while too many different colours, shapes and styles can create a chaotic, messy jumble. Less is definitely more. Simple schemes are also more manageable and mature more gracefully. To create unity and harmony, repeat the same plant groupings, colours, features and style throughout the garden. This gives your design coherence and creates a sense of rhythm and flow.

Focal points

Focal points are a crucial part of any garden design. They draw the eye, provide a 'pause point' for you to enjoy the garden from and help with styling of your chosen theme. All gardens should contain at least one focal point – without it, the space can seem lacking and uninspiring.

A focal point can be anything – a water feature, a sculpture or a striking container – basically something that is going to attract your attention and 'lead' you through the garden – something that stands out and says 'look at me'.

Plants can also make excellent focal points. When they are used in this way, we called them 'specimen plants'. A pot of brightly coloured tulips placed at the end

plants of equal volume. Alternatively, one large shrub in one border and three smaller ones in the opposite border can also give a balanced effect. Balance is particularly important in a formal garden (see pages 92–97) and symmetry helps to create this, for instance, marking a gateway or entrance with the same plant on either side. To get the most from your garden all year round, it is also worth considering the proportion of evergreens and deciduous shrubs you plant. Choosing these carefully can mean that your garden will have balance all year, and not look too bare in those colder months.

Creating a balance that works will give you a space that is unified.

▶ Evergreen topiary can create a year-round impact in your border.

▲ This sundial works as a strong focal point in its own right, but is enhanced by the striking planting that surround it, with just three plants and two colours used to make a bold statement.

of a path in spring can lead you to a pretty woodland area that might otherwise be missed. Alternatively, a single, strategically placed specimen tree, such as a Japanese maple (*Acer*), which becomes a fiery orange beacon in autumn; or a clump of dogwoods (*Cornus*), which produce a blaze of striking red, green or black stems in mid-winter; or a clipped piece of evergreen topiary, which becomes a statement piece in a long border throughout the year.

▶ Attractive containers make great focal points.

▲ Foliage can provide a dramatic colour palette.
▶ Using contrasting colours, like this orange and purple, can have a striking effect.

Making the link

Colour can be used to link your house to your garden. For instance, if you have an accent colour in your living room soft furnishings, you could carry this colour right through your garden, using it to draw your eye to key focal areas and divert your attention away from areas that are awaiting development.

Colour

Colour can change the whole mood of a garden, so it should be a major player in your wish list. Since it creates an emotional response, finding the right combinations can be a very personal process. Over the next few days, examine the effect certain colours have on you. Do you find the space you are in relaxing or stimulating, or does it make you feel restless? What shades and combinations are you drawn to, and why?

Remember, when choosing colours it is not just about the flowers, which have a relatively short lifespan. A well-designed planting scheme uses foliage, stems, bark and seedheads to create layers of colour all year round.

Colour-themed borders

When creating borders, you can restrict yourself to using just one colour – for instance, white (see pages 50–51 for a striking example). Such borders can be successful but you need to do some research to ensure there is year-round interest. Two-colour borders are a little easier as you can blend the two chosen colours to create a pleasing effect.

If you're planning a mixed colour border, concentrate on the shades used. Similar shades of pink, blue and purple look gorgeous together, as do shades of orange, red and yellow for something a bit more lively.

Using hot colours such as reds and oranges can be invigorating and uplifting, whereas using a cooler colour palette of purples, whites and greens would create an instantly restful feel. Pick your favourites and have a play. With a little planning your border could have some incredible vibrant combinations in spring and develop into something mellower as the season progresses into late summer.

Plant shapes

A plant's shape can be used to create different effects, and a combination of shapes will add interest and give a more three-dimensional feel to the space. However, don't overdo the variety. Trying to fit too many plant types and shapes in a border will create a chaotic effect. You will achieve much more impact if you limit your border to a maximum of seven different varieties and three main shapes. For example, large evergreen shrubs will create strong shapes. Having too many of these bold shapes can dominate a border, but complementing one with something softer and more mounding will add interest and unify the space. The same could be said when using lots of mounding, loosely formed plants – placing a more vertical shape amongst these will give a dynamic yet cohesive design.

Unless you're starting with mature trees and shrubs, most plants have yet to grow into their final shape, so it is worth doing a little research into how things will grow over the years as this will determine where you plant them.

Upright or columnar

Plants that are upright or column-shaped make great focal points and are best planted next to shapes that will show this off, like domes and mounds or something low and spreading. Like an exclamation mark through your borders, upright column-shaped plants draw the eye.

Arching

An arching form softens a border and creates a relaxed, informal effect. It also provides a sense of movement. If you want to create a naturalistic garden (see pages 106–115), arching plants are a must.

Fan-shaped

Often created by larger plants, a fan shape is dramatic, especially when the plant also has spear-like foliage, such as a *Phormium*. It is ideal for focal points. Use this shape sparingly, as drawing your eye to too many places at once can give a cluttered, restless feel.

Domes or mounds

These shapes really tie a border together. Generally, they are mid-height and the gentle mounds, which are planted between larger plants, often brush up against their neighbours.

Low and spreading

Plants that are low and spreading are good for linking planting areas together. They allow the eye to drift over them onto the next area and contrast well with upright, spiky plants.

▲ **A striking evergreen structure can create a bold focal point.**

▶ *Gypsophilas* **create a low, spreading effect to link different areas together.**

Upright or columnar plants
✽ Bamboos
✽ *Calamagrostis* 'Karl Foerster'
✽ *Cupressus sempervirens* 'Stricta' Group
✽ *Delphinium* 'Faust' and 'Cassius'
✽ *Digitalis purpurea* 'Alba'
✽ *Kniphofia* 'Nobilis'
✽ *Thuja occidentalis* 'Fastigiata'
✽ *Veronicastrum virginicum* 'Erica' and 'Fascination'

Fan-shaped plants
✽ *Eupatorium maculatum* Atropurpureum Group
✽ *Mahonia × media* 'Charity'
✽ *Matteuccia struthiopteris*
✽ *Miscanthus sinensis* 'Kaskade'
✽ *Phormium tenax*
✽ *Salvia × sylvestris* 'Dear Anja'
✽ *Salvia nemorosa* 'Lubecca'

Dome- or mound-shaped plants
✽ *Hakonechloa macra*
✽ *Hebe rakaiensis*
✽ *Hosta* (all varieties)
✽ *Lavandula* (all varieties)
✽ *Nepeta racemosa* 'Walker's Low'
✽ *Origanum laevigatum* 'Herrenhausen'
✽ *Sedum* 'Herbstfreude'
✽ *Stipa tenuissima*
✽ *Veronica longifolia* 'Blue John' or 'Lilac Fantasy'

Arching plants
✽ *Calamagrostis brachytricha* 'Mona'
✽ *Cephalaria radiata*
✽ *Dierama pulcherrimum*
✽ *Gladiolus communis* subsp. *byzantinus*
✽ *Molinia caerulea* subsp. *arundinacea* 'Cordoba' and 'Transparent'
✽ *Salvia* 'Indigo Spires'
✽ *Stipa gigantea* 'Gold Fontaene'

Low and spreading plants
✽ *Alchemilla mollis*
✽ *Erigeron karvinskianus*
✽ *Geranium* (all varieties)
✽ *Gypsophila repens* 'Filou White' and 'Rosa Schönheit'
✽ *Persicaria affinis*
✽ *Stachys byzantina*
✽ *Thymus* (all varieties)

▶ *Erigeron karvinskianus* **creates a wonderful, low, tumbling form.**

Texture

The texture of plants is something rarely considered by the novice gardener, but different leaf and flower textures can really bring your border to life. For instance, you can brighten a dark corner with a glossy-leaved shrub, such as laurel (*Laurus nobilis*), as the foliage reflects light. The fine foliage of a Japanese maple (*Acer*) creates a delicate and pretty effect, while the soft, furry silver leaves of lamb's ears (*Stachys byzantina*) have a wonderful tactile quality. Velvety petals make a border appear richer and more luxurious.

To create a vibrant feel, create combinations of plants with differing textures – for instance, plants with smooth leaves alongside plants that have hairy foliage, or large, bold foliage beside small, intricate leaves. Textural contrasts are particularly effective at the front of a border, where they can be seen and enjoyed most easily.

Great plants for building interesting texture

- *Acer griseum*
- *Acer japonicum*
- *Astilbe*
- *Betula papyrifera*
- *Briza media*
- *Fatsia japonica*
- *Hakonechloa macra*
- *Hosta* (all varieties)
- *Stachys byzantina*
- *Stipa* (all varieties)
- *Mahonia × media*
- *Pennisetum*
- *Phlomis fruticosa*
- *Phyllostachys*
- *Santolina chamaecyparissus*
- *Sedum* (all varieties)
- *Sempervivum*

▲ The reflective, glossy leaves of the laurel can brighten shadowy corners in your border.

◄ Delicate Aster foliage next to reflective water feels restful.

▲ Hostas are great for building up texture.

Border size and shape

Whatever the size of your garden, the bigger and deeper the borders, the better. A deep bed will make a far greater impact than a narrow border, as you will have room to plant a wider variety of plants and layer the planting. Layering interest is achieved by planting under shrubs with bulbs, planting climbers up trees and into shrubs, repetition of colour and form within a border, and having the room to plant taller things at the back of a border and tier down the heights of plants towards the front. This looks much more interesting than having a single row of plants standing to attention cheek by jowl. Fewer big borders will have a much better overall look than lots of smaller ones.

▲ Tiered planting gives a border shape and form from front to back.

▶ Curved borders create a flowing effect that draws you into the garden.

Straight borders

Straight-edged borders can look very formal. To make the most of them, embrace this and keep formality in the planting too. This is best achieved by restricting the number of plant varieties, shapes and colours you use. If you like this look, you can take the theme further by creating a formal garden made up mainly of evergreens (see pages 92–97).

If formal isn't really your style, but you have no choice other than to have a straight border because of your existing hard landscaping, break up the line with plants that creep onto the path and blur the edge to look more relaxed.

Curved borders

I prefer curved borders. They invite you to wander through a garden, as you're unable to see the entire border by standing at one end. A curved line causes your eye to stop and enjoy what is at the bend before you move on and discover what lies beyond it. Gentle curves are easy on the eye, whereas sudden, stronger curves can have a bolder effect. Think about the effect you want to achieve – soft and gentle or bold and striking – and plant accordingly for that 'wow' factor.

Corner beds

If you have a triangular bed, work with it and try to imagine you are making it a three dimensional triangle with your plants. Use taller things at the back and in the centre, then work towards the front of your triangle, gradually lowering the height of the plants you choose. Using this technique can also be effective in a long border – you just repeat the sequence of planting in triangles down the whole length of a border, blending the gaps with gentle domes and hummocks that let the eye pause along the space. This gives great rhythm and unity.

Designing your garden

Now it's time for you to think about where to position all the different elements. The following two chapters include detailed information on using plants (see pages 40–67) and creating specific garden styles (see pages 68–139), but first you need to consider the bigger picture and draw up a plan of your garden.

Drawing up a planting plan

First go out with a tape measure and measure everything, including your boundaries and where your house sits within your plot. You also need to mark on anything that won't be moved, such as mature trees or existing hard landscaping.

Next, transfer your measurements onto paper by drawing a very simple plan of your garden using a scale ruler. This makes what had seemed like a huge, frightening task into a piece of paper where you can doodle and get creative! This way you can work out how and where all the elements are going to fit into the space and experiment with your design ideas without wasting money or hours of labour. Just drawing this simple plan will help you to work out where best to position your new flower beds and borders. Keep making adjustments until you're happy with the result.

Keep or start again?

Trying to incorporate what you have in terms of landscaping will obviously save you money. However, you may find that moving away from the existing landscaping will give you greater scope for expression, allowing you to design the garden that works best for you.

Legal constraints

Before starting any work in your garden, check for any legal constraints that might get in your way. Going ahead and finding out when it's too late can be a costly mistake that is very easily avoided.

1 Conservation areas and sites of scientific interest – These are all subject to restrictions and any changes must go through the right authorities. A quick phone call to your local council will tell you if your garden sits in such a site.

2 Tree preservation orders – Disturbing a tree that has a tree preservation order on it is against the law, even if the tree is on your land. The local council can tell you if you have any listed trees on your property. You must ask permission before any work is carried out on or around the tree.

3 Boundaries and fences – The deeds of the property will tell you where the boundaries lie and who is responsible for which boundary. It may be that you have to ask a neighbour's permission to put up or change a fence or wall.

4 Front gardens – Since 2008 you must gain planning permission if you want to install 5 square metres or more of impermeable surface in your front garden. This is because tarmac and concrete do not absorb excess rainwater, resulting in flooding of roads and pavements.

Chapter 2

Choosing and using plants

There are many important elements in a garden, but it is the plants that are most important. They give your garden character, and their shape, colour and texture, and the way they interact, really bring the space to life. So it's important to spend time on choosing your plants, and deciding how you're going to use them to their best effect.

It takes
all kinds...

Your chosen style and theme will affect which elements you want to use the most. Many people want their garden to have interest for as much of the year as possible, which can be achieved by using a good cross section of trees, shrubs, herbaceous plants and bulbs, plus the odd annual. However, that doesn't mean you have to follow this approach. If you like roses, use lots of them! Extend their interest by buying ones that will give you hips in the winter and underplanting them with a carpet of crocuses, winter aconites and anemones to brighten up the area in the spring.

Whichever style or theme you choose, always position the largest plants first. This will create a skeleton – the backbone of your design if you like. Shrubs are the muscle, the stuff that anchors the rest of the border's components together, like perennials, annuals and bulbs. Whatever you choose to use, flesh out your design by growing under, growing up, and repeat planting. This will make up for periods where the main players are dormant and also give your garden body.

▲ Rose hips for winter interest.

Trees

Trees are the most prominent plants in the garden, and add structure and height to planting schemes. They are on show all year and give the garden a feeling of maturity – an anchor for all the other plants within the space.

Selecting the right tree is crucial. Before choosing, check its eventual height and spread as it must be in proportion to your garden. Also, choose one that you really love and will give you as much pleasure as possible. Large and very long-lived, trees are not easy to move or replace.

Trees for small gardens

If you have a small garden your choice of tree is particularly important, as you may be able to accommodate only one. Also, as it will be a prominent feature in a small space it needs to earn its keep so should have several seasons of interest. I particularly love mountain ash (*Sorbus*, see page 125). These trees produce blossom in spring, their pinnate leaves have the most spectacular autumn colour, and the clusters of berries in winter range from ruby red and blush pink to golden tones of orange. They make me think of dangly jewelled earrings. Pinnate leaves, when you look closely, are comprised of several small leaves or leaflets sharing a common stalk.

Multi-stemmed trees make great feature plants, especially if you pick one with interesting bark such as the Tibetan cherry (*Prunus serrula*), which has peeling red bark that looks like fragments of stained glass when backlit in autumn and winter. *Acer griseum* is another tree with fantastic peeling orange-brown tactile bark, making it popular for winter interest. Another tree for winter interest and a favourite with landscape architects is the birch *Betula utilis* var. *jacquemontii*. Its white stems are very striking and its foliage is delicate, so it casts only light shade and has lovely movement.

Just like plants, trees have varied shapes. These shapes range from goblet, columnar, pyramidal, round and oval. Considering the mature shape of a tree is vital when positioning your tree – you don't want it to block an important view or have its growth stunted due to it being too close to a building. Mirroring the shape of your tree with the odd plant shape or specimen shrub is another subtle way to make your borders feel more considered and cohesive.

◀ Small trees in a front garden can bring balance.

▼ The peeling bark of a Tibetan cherry tree.

▲ *Betula jacquemontii* trees have stunning bark.

▲ *Lavandula* flowers
all summer and is
very low maintenance.
◀ *Cotinus coggyria* has
spectacular plum-
coloured foliage.

Shrubs

Shrubs are a large and varied group of
plants. All have woody stems that do
not die back so, like trees, they provide
the permanent framework of a planting
scheme and are an invaluable 'backing
vocal' for your garden. Most shrubs
have a bushy habit but sizes vary
greatly, from good old lavender
measuring in at an average of 40cm
to something like a mock orange

(*Philadelphus coronarius*) that can reach
up to 3 metres. As with trees, it's
important to make sure you look at the
eventual size that your shrub will grow
to as you don't want it to outgrow the
space. Some shrubs can be cut back
really hard every year, which will
restrict their growth and keep them at
a height that suits your border.

Attractive foliage

You may choose shrubs for their
beautiful leaf shape or colour.
Evergreen shrubs, which retain their
leaves throughout the year, can provide
winter interest, as well as giving
screening for privacy and providing
shelter from wind and noise. *Euonymus*
is a particularly reliable evergreen and
there are many different foliage
variations, including gold- and silver-
variegated forms. They tolerate shade
and can be clipped regularly.

Deciduous shrubs lose their leaves
in autumn and have bare branches over
winter. However, they compensate for
this by producing fresh new growth in

Pruning flowering

A common rule of thumb with a
shrub is to prune it immediately
after it has finished flowering.
However, this is not always the
case and keeping a record of
what you have planted is always
advisable so you can check how it
should be maintained.

spring, a mass of leaves in summer, and autumn colour before they fall. Smoke bush (*Cotinus coggygria* 'Royal Purple', see page 86), for instance, has spectacular plum foliage and long, frothy pink panicles in summer.

Flowering shrubs

Many shrubs – both evergreen and deciduous – produce beautiful flowers. There are flowers for every season of the year – for instance, you might want to include a rhododendron in spring, a buddleia (*Buddleja*) in summer, a hydrangea in autumn or witch hazel (*Hamamelis*) in winter.

Flowering shrubs are often highly fragrant. For instance, mock orange (*Philadelphus*) and honeysuckle (*Lonicera*) have a wonderful heady scent in summer, while Christmas box (*Sarcococca confusa*) has deliciously scented winter flowers.

After flowering, many shrubs produce brightly coloured berries or fruits, which look very attractive and provide a vital food source for birds in autumn to help them build up their reserves in winter. *Berberis*, *Cotoneaster* and *Viburnum* are tough, versatile shrubs that produce an abundance of colourful berries.

▲ *Buddleja* **is a great flowering shrub that will attract butterflies.**
▼ **Varieties of Euonymus give year-round colour.**
▼ *Hamamelis* × *intermedia* **(witch hazel).**

Climbing plants

Climbers are plants that have adapted to growing through other plants and up vertical surfaces. They are super useful, whatever size garden you have, as they can scramble up high and grow in awkward places that other plants cannot reach, and add a splash of colour to stark walls, fences and dull trees and shrubs. This makes them particularly useful in smaller gardens.

Self-supporting climbers

Climbers can be used in many different ways and come in many different forms. Some climbing plants, such as climbing hydrangea (*Hydrangea anomala* subsp. *petiolaris*) and ivy (*Hedera*), have roots that will attach to a surface they are given to climb up, whether that be a wall or a fence – all you need to do is provide a host for them to climb up and they will do the rest themselves. Both of these plants are evergreen, so provide year-round coverage.

Twining climbers

Other climbers, such as clematis and honeysuckle (*Lonicera*), twine and twist around their support and need a little more help initially, such as attaching wires or a trellis to the wall. They will also need tying in to start with, but once they're established they will do the rest themselves.

Alternatively, you can encourage them to scramble up trees and large shrubs. Using the frame of a host plant when it is not in flower can extend its season of interest. One of my favourite ways to use climbers is to plant roses up trees – once they reach maturity they look magnificent. And sweet peas (*Lathyrus odoratus*) are simply a must. A word of caution: highly vigorous climbers can overwhelm their host plant, so it is important to do some research and match the strength of the climber to its host tree or shrub.

▲ Climbers, such as this beautiful *Wisteria floribunda* 'Alba', can provide areas of shade in your garden.
▶ *Hydrangea anomola* subsp. *Petiolaris* (top) and a beautiful *Clematis* (bottom).

Planting climbers

When planting a climber, always dig a hole at least 30cm away from the base of the wall or fence. If you plant it any closer the soil will be very dry because of the 'rainshadow' effect. Also, house walls can be dry at the base because the foundations and brickwork absorb moisture from the soil. Leave any canes in place and lean the plant towards its support.

▶ *Fritillaria meleagris* has distinctive chequered petals.

▶▶ Here, irises have been planted under a *Cercis canadensis* (forest pansy), a deciduous shrub or small tree.

◀ *Helenium* adds striking colour to a border.

When to plant

The best time to plant herbaceous perennials is autumn or early spring, when they are dormant. Planting at these times causes the plants less stress and allows them to become established in their new environment before they dazzle you with their wonderful floral displays.

Herbaceous perennials

Herbaceous perennials are plants that are left in the ground from year to year and have a long-lived root system, yet they are not woody like trees and shrubs. They produce fresh stems, leaves and flowers every year. They look fantastic from early to late summer, but then the growth dies back underground in winter to re-emerge in spring – a bit like plant hibernation.

Ranging in height from low-growing soil-huggers to tall sun worshippers, and with every colour, texture and leaf shape imaginable, the options with herbaceous plants are endless. In my opinion, they are the most valuable plant group.

Herbaceous and mixed borders

Traditionally, herbaceous perennials are grown on their own in a herbaceous border. However, these are often high maintenance and not suitable in a small garden as there is nothing to look at in winter once they've died down. Today they are more commonly planted in mixed borders, where they make ideal partners for other plants – growing under trees, between shrubs and over bulbs. They suit both formal and informal schemes. Herbaceous plants are extremely hardworking and most will flower for a long period of time if dead-headed.

Using herbaceous perennials

There are a wealth of herbaceous perennials out there to choose from. Whether you want some strong architectural leaves to draw the eye to a focal point, some wonderful textures of foliage to create a tapestry of plants in the shade, or masses of flowers for the summer months, you will not be short of inspiration and choice when looking at this fantastic group of plants.

Bulbs

The term 'bulb' is a loose one, generally used to describe true bulbs, corms, tubers and rhizomes. These all differ slightly, but what they have in common is that they all have a fleshy underground storage organ. This stores up energy when the plant is dormant and then releases it when it is needed for the new season of growth. They survive in hostile conditions so they are generally resilient, undemanding plants.

Bulbs are great for borders, under deciduous trees and shrubs in spring, and in containers, which you can move around the garden to provide colour where you need it.

Using bulbs in borders
Although most bulbs are planted in autumn and winter to bloom in early spring, there are flowers for all seasons – including winter.

After flowering, bulbs will die back and come again the following year. Some bulbs are very reliable, such as daffodils (*Narcissus*), crocuses and snowdrops (*Galanthus*), while others like tulips (*Tulipa*) and irises can be a little more temperamental, so choose your varieties carefully.

Some of my personal favourites are snakeshead fritillaries (*Fritillaria meleagris*) – I just love their fine stems and foliage with the chequered petals. I also love alliums in all their forms, but especially *Allium aflatunense* with their purple pompoms that seem to float above borders suspended like purple planets.

Bulb foliage

The one downside to bulbs is the foliage that is often left once the flowers are past their best. While it can be tempting to cut off the leaves, it's very important to leave them alone for at least six weeks before you cut them back. This gives the plant time to photosynthesise, re-charging the bulb so it is able to flower again next year.

Annuals and tender perennials

Annuals have a one-year life span, so they flower, seed and die all in the same year. This is usually because they are not hardy and are unable to cope with winter. They usually start growing in spring, flower in summer and die in autumn. *Lobelia*, petunias and tobacco plants (*Nicotiana*) are some popular examples of these plants.

There are also plants that we often treat as annuals but are actually tender perennials. We tend to buy them afresh each year, plant them as summer bedding and then discard them at the end of the season, as they can't survive heavy frost. However, in warmer climates tender perennials would happily go on for years. You can keep some alive by bringing them in to a cool room indoors or a heated greenhouse over winter – try this with fuchsias, penstemons and verbena.

Summer bedding

Annuals and tender perennials are great border fillers and are the quickest and best way to introduce colour into your garden. They are informal pretties that, if used correctly, are a brilliant stopgap between your spring and late summer interest. Choose plants that tie in with your existing scheme in terms of colour and style; some have a lovely fragrance too. The great thing about these short-lived plants is if your border design doesn't work out as you had hoped it doesn't matter – you just discard them and experiment with something new the following season.

Annuals work especially well in a cottage garden (see pages 70–79) and their often-graceful stems are fantastic for weaving in and out of more sturdy herbaceous perennials. They are often allowed to self-seed, which gives a random, ad hoc feel to a garden. Poppies (*Papaver somniferum*), cornflowers (*Centaurea cyanus*) and cosmos create a lovely hazy look redolent of a wildflower meadow.

Annuals and tender perennials can also be a great addition to your containers – try begonias, pelargoniums and zinnias.

▲ Annual poppies help create the feel of a wildflower meadow.

◀ *Cosmos* is a good example of a tender perennial.

▶ This *Salvia* 'Hot Lips' is another good tender perennial.

Perfume

Even though it is an invisible factor, fragrance should be high on our agenda of things to incorporate into a border.

Try to identify what scents you like and think about how to use them to best effect. For instance, you might like to place a pot of lavender (*Lavandula*) by the back door so that when you brush past it after a hard day at work you will get that soothing hit as its aroma is released. Alternatively, you might like to plant summer jasmine (*Jasminum officinale*) near a seating area so you can breathe in its heady fragrance while you relax. Often, the showiest blooms don't have a strong scent as they already attract pollinating insects and therefore don't have to 'try' in other ways. Adding another layer of interest to an area using scent is something often overlooked, but it really shouldn't be, and spreading the scent through the seasons in your garden will give you even more enjoyment.

If you plan carefully you can enjoy fragrant plants in your garden every season of the year. Many plants that flower in winter have a beautiful fragrance – for instance, Christmas box (*Sarcococca confusa*), *Mahonia* and *Viburnum* × *bodnantense* smell incredible at a time when little else is going on in the garden – a real treat during those cold days.

Alpines

Also known as rock plants, alpines are a group of miniature, mat-forming hardy perennials, dwarf trees and shrubs, and bulbs that originate in the mountains. They usually flower for a relatively short period in spring and early summer, producing delicate, clear-coloured blooms, but some are evergreen and provide year-round interest. Often overlooked, alpines are really tough little plants and will tolerate a very low level of maintenance once established.

Maintaining a rockery

Water the plants in your rockery regularly in the first few months until established, and always top-dress the whole area with alpine grit or 10mm gravel. This will lock in moisture, keep the weeds down and add to the scree effect of alpines' natural habitat.

Creating a rockery

Alpines are often grown in rock gardens, or rockeries. These go in and out of fashion – they sometimes get a bit of a groan when mentioned in gardening circles – but I love them. If you're lucky enough to have a rockery you want to revamp, or you would like to create one from scratch, do it! As long as your site gets a good level of sun and is free draining you can grow alpines.

Plant the rockery as you would a mixed border – combine plants for height and structure and contrast them with lower, mat-forming plants and flowering bulbs such as miniature tulips (*Tulipa*) and daffodils (*Narcissus*). Many alpine plants cling, creep and tumble, which gives a lovely natural effect. You will find over time that plants self-seed in crevices where you could never have managed to plant them yourself, which adds to the charm.

▲ Using boulders gives your alpines something to grow amongst, against and over.

Ferns

Ferns are fantastic at growing in the most difficult of areas, whether that be dry shade, damp shade, in an old tree stump or the crevice of a wall that gets no light. A fern on its own will tend to look a little lost, so plant a few varieties for a good effect. My favourites for dry shade are *Polystichum setiferum* 'Divisilobum Wollaston' and *Dryopteris filix-mas* 'Linearis Polydactyla'. Damp shade lovers like *Adiantum pedatum* and *Matteuccia struthiopteris* are wonderful at providing texture, and *Asplenium scolopendrium*, known as hart's-tongue fern, will grow just about anywhere.

Grasses

A garden can never have too many grasses. Their biggest appeal for me is their movement and ability to create a naturalistic aesthetic. They look just as good planted in large groups as they do dotted throughout a border, and some specimen grasses such as *Molinia caerula* subsp. *arundinacea* 'Cordoba' make great focal points. They also add some fantastic metallic bronze and gold tones to a garden, which you get from few other plants. If you ever want to divide your grasses (see page 153) do this in early spring, as many dislike autumn division and you may weaken the plant.

▲ Some ferns can get big, so consider your space.

▲ Striking purple foliage against lime green ferns.

▲ *Stipa gigantea* is another great grass for a focal point.

Setting out your plants

Whether you're designing a garden from scratch in a particular style (see Chapter 3, pages 68–139) or simply adding plants to an existing border, you'll need to think about how you're going to arrange them. Here are some border styles to consider – if this is your first attempt at planting a border, the styles listed here will help you create something that is right for you. Many designers have a style all of their own, or pick and choose from the styles listed here to create a unique signature look, so if you're feeling creative and confident, why not do the same?

▲ Underplanting with bulbs like these alliums creates added interest in a mixed border.

◀ **Using garden canes to mark out the bed for planting.**

Matrix planting

This is a method of planting I direct many novice gardeners towards; it's a foolproof way of filling a mixed border without over-planting.

After preparing the soil for planting (see page 142), lay garden canes out flat on the ground in a grid of roughly 1m squares.

If you're planting a mixed border, start with your shrubs. On all plant labels it should tell you the mature height and spread of the plant. Let's take a *Viburnum tinus* 'Eve Price'. I know this will fill at least one of my metre squares, so I will plant just one plant in one square. I might then want to grow *Calamagrostis × acutiflora* 'Karl Foerster', which is quite compact, so it would take three mature plants to fill a metre square. Then it would take five *Astrantia minor* 'Moulin Rouge' to fill another. Get the idea?

Seeing the space divided up like this seems to make it much easier to get your head around how many plants are needed and where they should go. If you can't afford to plant semi-mature shrubs it may take a few years to really see how this method works, but once things have grown up to one another and the edges are a little blurred you will never see the original block pattern, as no plant I know will grow in a perfect square!

Mixed border

A mixed border is the most common way to set out plants. As the name suggests, mixed borders incorporate a little bit of everything. The permanent structure comes mainly from trees and shrubs, so it's best to choose ones that will work hard for you. Herbaceous perennials and annuals thread through the border linking the areas together and shrubs are underplanted with bulbs and spring-flowering plants. Where possible, choose trees and shrubs with several seasons of interest – for instance, flowers, fruit and autumn colour.

A good starting point is to create a table of all the plants you want to grow and then divide the table into a list of months. You can then see what flowers when and if this is spread evenly over the year or has the heaviest flush when you are most likely to use the garden. You can also consider good planting combinations.

▲ Using similar colours but different flower forms next to each other adds texture and depth to a mixed border.

Planting in swathes

To achieve a natural look, dividing your borders into swathes, drifts and masses is the way to go. To achieve a swathe, plant in irregular, organic shapes that merge into one another. Use multiples of the same plants within each shape at variable planting distances.

Many contemporary gardeners use this method and I adore the look and feel of such a border if done correctly. The best results come when you have really considered the times of year when plants will flower as then you can play with heights. The best example I can give you of this method is this: if I

had a border with swathes of the same plant threaded through the area, early in the year I may have it full of diamond grass (*Calamagrostis brachytricha*). This has great early foliage, which grows up to 60cm and is a brilliant vibrant backdrop for plants like *Agastache*, which often has a blue or purple fluffy spire of flowers and will pop up through the grass, or *Thalictrum*, which has delicate lacy foliage and flowers that provide a great contrast to the smooth spears of the diamond grass foliage. Later in the season, once the *Thalictrum* is past its best, the grass will flower and can be joined by

Veronicastrum, with its perfect whorls of foliage you will never have noticed until its tall elegant flowering spires appear. This gives two very different looks to one bed at different stages of the year.

With careful planning, you can change the whole colour scheme of a border from one season to the next, just by considering the time of year that plants will flower together. This attention to detail is what takes planting design to the next level and will give your border the 'wow factor'.

▶ The delicate lacy foliage and flowers of *Thalictrum*.

▼ Planting in swathes creates a natural and varied look all year round – here is an autumn example.

Dove Cottage

Prairie planting

This is a style of planting that has been in vogue for quite a few years. It consists of a mixture of grasses and robust flowering perennials and is intended to mimic how plants grow in a large open area as they would in a prairie. Plants in the wild usually spread their seed very closely to where the parent plant originally grew, giving large clumps of the same plant that colonise the same area. Every so often a rogue seed will have travelled a little further along and started growing amongst something else quite unexpectedly.

For instance, you could place a huge clump of grasses of a single variety like *Andropogon gerardii* 'Prairie Sommer' and groups of the low, ground-creeping plant *Scutellaria incana* in front of it, with *Erigeron annuus* dotted here and there to look as though they have self-seeded (which they eventually will, adding to the overall effect). Trying to create space between the heights of your plants and the clusters of your plants themselves will help you to achieve this look.

If you have the space, prairie planting can look very attractive. It will take some trial and error and a few years to get right but is very effective when it works. It is also low maintenance, as it should be a very informal and relaxed expanse of garden and will manage itself once mature. Keeping on top of the weeds until the plants are mature is important, then it just needs to be all cut back to the ground in early spring.

◀ **Self-seeding plants create a hazy feel.**

Be restrained

Whichever planting scheme you choose, you can make it work for your space by adding more of the same variety of plants or reducing numbers. Try not to over complicate by adding lots of different types of plants, as the result can be messy. Remember, three of the same plant will give more impact than three different varieties dotted in a border.

Monoblock planting

Whatever size your bed, this approach can look brilliant and very modern if done the right way – but it's not for the faint-hearted. Just consider the proportions of plant to bed to achieve the best results. A few small raised beds in a front garden, each planted up with a different variety of grasses, can be just as effective as huge borders of the same plant in the biggest of gardens. One of the best examples I have seen of monoblock planting is at Scampston Hall, near the North Yorkshire coast. Here the legendary plantsman Piet Oudolf has planted huge waved beds of *Molinia caerulea* subsp. *caerulea* 'Poul Petersen' – and nothing else (pictured). This is a wonderful, hardy grass with an almost purple tinge to the flower, and planted together on this scale it looks very contemporary yet extremely restful, just a sea of gentle movement and green. In autumn the plant turns a beautiful buff brown. There is very little maintenance needed, as the plants are all the same.

Sourcing plants

Where to buy plants

Once you've drawn up your list it's very likely you'll have to go to several different places to get everything on it.

Garden centres

Not all garden centres are able to offer a huge range of plants, especially when it comes to more specialist varieties, so you might not be able to find everything that you need at your local garden centre. They are a reliable place to visit, though, for equipment and supplies such as fertiliser and compost.

Specialist nurseries and the internet

Buying from a dedicated plant nursery can be a very rewarding experience. People who own nurseries are very knowledgeable about what they grow and will be able to advise you. If you can find a local nursery, all the better, as the plants will have been grown in conditions similar to those in your garden. Many specialist nurseries are online and will send plants by mail order. This is a great way to track down a particular plant you're looking for.

Plant fairs and flower shows

These places are bursting with inspiration and are full of the most passionate people in the industry who love what they do – so take full advantage. Make sure you have a notepad and pen or charged phone or tablet to hand, as it's impossible to remember all the things you see and like. Take pictures and make notes of any names of plants you think might work at home. The show gardens are a great place to start for inspiration, while the floral marquees are

Acquiring new plants is a real pleasure, but for the pleasure to last you need to choose plants that will perform well in your garden. It is all too easy to become over-excited by all the treats on offer at a garden centre or nursery and you can end up going home with lots of beautiful plants that might not be suitable. It's best to go with a list of plants you would like and where you intend to put them – that way, if you are offered an alternative you can check it against the conditions of the area in which it will be planted.

wonderful to see and a fantastic place to get hold of the latest plant varieties.

Superstores

Many supermarkets and DIY stores sell plants and you can often get some pretty good deals. It is always worth being cautious though. These plants have a short shelf life and have often been imported from nurseries abroad. Always check that the soil is moist. If you see roots at the bottom of the pot this is a good sign that the plant has an established root system that will help it cope in its new environment when planted.

When to buy

Although container-grown plants are generally available throughout the year, some plants, such as hedging plants and roses, are sold bare-rooted in winter. Bare-rooted is when the plant is lifted out of its growing site, the plant is pruned and the roots are put into a polythene bag and sent out to customers. Not only are they less expensive, bare-rooted plants also tend to grow away more quickly and perform better in their new positions in the garden. Bare-rooted plants survive being out of the soil for a short time in their period of dormancy, but it is best to plant them as soon as possible after purchase.

Buying herbaceous perennials late in the season

If you happen to buy herbaceous perennials when they are past their best at the end of the flowering season, take them home and immediately divide each plant into smaller clumps, using a hand fork to pull the roots apart. This will give you three plants for the price of one. It is also beneficial for the plant, as if it has been in the garden centre all summer, it will be bursting out of its pot and desperate to spread its roots. Plant your divided plants in a separate planting hole and water well. They will grow the following season and get just as big as the original you bought, provided the plant is suited to the conditions where it has been planted. This gives you much more impact and a greater show of flowers.

▲ A bare-rooted plant.

At-a-glance plant lists

Plants suited to hot and dry environments

Allium cernuum
Anthemis tinctoria
Buxus
Ceanothus
Cercis siliquastrum
Cistus × purpureus
Cordyline australis
Diascia
Echinops ritro
Eryngium
Festuca glauca
Ficus carica
Geranium cinereum
   'Ballerina'
Geranium pyrenaicum
   'Bill Wallis'
Jasminum officinale
Juniperus
Lavandula
Nandina domestica
Osteospermum
Papaver orientale
Passiflora caerulea
Pelargonium
Perovskia
Phlomis purpurea
Pinus
Santolina
   chamaecyparissus
Sedum (all varieties)
Stipa gigantea
Trachycarpus

Plants suited to damp and shady environments

Actaea simplex
Aruncus dioicus
Brunnera macrophylla
Camellia japonica
Cornus alba
Darmera peltata
Digitalis
Dryopteris filix-mas
Eranthis hyemalis
Fatsia japonica
Helleborus orientalis
Hosta (all varieties)
Hydrangea quercifolia
Luzula sylvatica
Matteuccia struthiopteris
Mitella breweri
Osmunda regalis
Polystichum setiferum
Rodgersia
Ranunculus
Sarcococca hookeriana
Thalictrum delavayi

Plants suited to dry shade

Ajuga reptans
Anemone nemorosa
Asplenium scolopendrium
Bergenia
Brunnera macrophylla
Clematis montana
Cotoneaster salicifolius
Cyclamen hederifolium
Deschampsia cespitosa
Epimedium × rubrum
Euonymus fortunei
Euphorbia amygdaloides
Geranium macrorrhizum
Geranium nordstrum
Geranium phaeum
Hakonechloa macra
Hedera helix
Ilex aquifolium
Luzula sylvatica
Osmanthus delavayi
Pachysandra terminalis
Sambucus nigra
Sarcococca confusa
Skimmia japonica
Taxus baccata
Viburnum davidii
Vinca minor

Plants suited to exposed sites

Achillea
Alchemilla mollis
Anemone × hybrida
Aquilegia vulgaris
Armeria maritima
Aubretia
Aucuba japonica
Berberis
Buddleja
Calluna vulgaris
Cotoneaster
Crataegus monogyna
Elaeagnus × ebbingei
Erica
Erigeron
Eryngium
Eschscholzia californica
Euonymus japonicus
Griselinia littoralis
Hebe
Helianthemum
Ilex aquifolium
Juniperus
Mahonia
Rosa rugosa
Salix purpurea
Sedum
Taxus baccata
Viburnum

Low-maintenance plants

Alliums
Bergenia
Brunnera
Buxus sempervirens
Camellia
Daffodils
Dicentra
Digitalis
Fatsia japonica
Ferns (all varieties)
Galanthus
Geraniums (all varieties)
Hebe
Hellebores (all varieties)
Hydrangea petiolaris
Ilex crenata
Kniphofia
Lonicera nitida
Molinia (all varieties)
Penstemon
Persicaria amplexicaulis
Phormium
Pieris
Rosemary
Rudbeckia var. sullivantii 'Goldsturm'
Salvia
Sarcococca confusa
Sedum (all varieties)
Sempervivums
Skimmia japonica
Stipa (all varieties)
Taxus baccata

Scented plants

Actaea japonica
Choisya
Clematis montana
Daphne
Dianthus
Euphorbia mellifera
Jasminum nudiflorum
Lavendula
Lilium candidum
Lonicera fragrantissima
Magnolia grandiflora
Mahonia japonica
Monarda
Osmanthus × burkwoodii
Philadelphus
Phlox maculata
Rhododendron 'Fragrantissimum'
Roses (all varieties)
Sarcococca hookeriana
Sweet peas
Thymus
Trachelospermum jasminoides
Viburnum × bodnantense
Wisteria floribunda

Textured plants

Acer griseum
Acer palmatum
Aruncus
Astilbe
Betula papyrifera
Briza media
Cardoon
Cordyline
Coreopsis
Echinops
Eryngium
Festuca glauca
Hakonechloa macra
Hosta (all varieties)
Mahonia
Pelargonium
Pennisetum
Perovskia
Phormium
Pinus
Pulsatilla vulgaris
Salvia
Santolina chamaecyparissus
Sedums (all varieties)
Stachys byzantina
Stipa tenuissima

Feature/Architectural plants

Acanthus mollis
Acer (all varieties)
Amelanchier lamarckii
Betula jacquemontii
Calamagrostis × acutiflora 'Karl Foerster'
Cornus alternifolia
Cynara cardunculus
Delphinium (all varieties)
Dicksonia antarctica
Eremurus robustus
Gunnera manicata
Kniphofia
Molinia
Molinia caerulea subsp. arundinacea
Phlomis tuberosa
Phormium
Phyllostachys aurea
Phyllostachys nigra
Rudbeckia laciniata 'Herbstsonne'
Stipa gigantea
Trachycarpus fortunei
Verbascum olympicum
Yucca

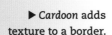
▶ **Cardoon** adds texture to a border.

Berrying plants

Callicarpa bodinieri
Clerodendrum
    trichotomum
Cornus canadensis
Cotoneaster
Crataegus monogyna
Decaisnea fargesii
Euonymus europaeus
Gaultheria mucronata
Hippophae rhamnoides
Leycesteria formosa
Malus
Prunus padus
Pyracantha
Rosa rugosa
Sambucus
Skimmia japonica
Sorbus
Taxus baccata
Viburnum davidii
Viburnum opulus

Bulbs for all seasons

Alliums
Anemone
Camassia
Chionodoxa
Crocus
Cyclamen
Eranthis
Erythronium
Fritillaria
Galanthus
Hyacinthoides non-scripta
Iris reticulata
Lilium
Narcissus
Nectaroscordum
Nerine
Scilla
Tulipa

Trees for small gardens

Acer griseum
Acer pseudoplatanus
    'Brilliantissimum'
Amelanchier alnifolia
    'Obelisk'
Betula utilis
Cercidiphyllum
    japonicum
Cercis canadensis
Crataegus persimilis
Hamamelis × intermedia
Liquidambar styraciflua
Magnolia stellata
Prunus (all varieties)
Sorbus pseudovilmorinii
Tilia cordata

Plants for screening and hedging

Aucuba
Berberis
Buxus sempervirens
Carpinus betulus
Cotoneaster lacteus
Crataegus monogyna
Escallonia
Euonymus japonicus
Fagus sylvatica
Griselinia littoralis
Ilex aquifolium
Laurus nobilis
Lonicera nitida
Osmanthus
Photinia × fraseri
Phyllostachys
Prunus spinosa
Taxus baccata
Thuja

Pollution-tolerant plants

Aubretia
Aucuba japonica
Berberis
Bergenia
Brachyglottis
Buddleja
Camellia
Clematis montana
Choisya
Colchicum
Cordyline
Fargesia
Festuca glauca
Geranium (all varieties)
Hakonechloa
Hebe (all varieties)
Heuchera (all varieties)
Hosta (all varieties)
Ilex aquifolium
Juniperus
Kniphofia
Lavendula
Phormium
Pieris japonica
Sambucus
Sedum
Spirea
Stipa tenuissima

Annuals and tender perennials for all seasons

Ammi majus
Briza maxima
Calendula
Centaurea cyanus
Cerinthe major
Cleome
Cosmos
Dahlia
Eschscholzia californica
Helianthus
Heliotrope
Lathyrus odoratus
Nasturtium
Nicotiana sylvestris
Nigella
Orlaya
Panicum elegans
Papaver
Pelargonium
Rudbeckia
Salvia 'Indigo Spires'
Verbena
Verbena bonariensis
Zinnia

◄ *Verbena* is good for temporary screening at the height of summer.

Chapter 3

Garden styles: create the look

I've already talked about reflecting your style and personality in your garden. One of the ways you can do this, while still making sure your garden works as a whole, is by choosing an overall garden style to adopt. In this chapter I'll introduce you to some of the main styles and show how you can create them using particular plants.

Romantic cottage garden

Quintessentially English, cottage gardens are romantic and full of charm. The cottage garden style goes back to Edwardian times and was a reaction to the formal and structured gardening that was in fashion at that time. Sometimes both flowers and vegetables would be grown together, all adding to the dreamy haphazard effect. Today, flowers are the key component of the cottage garden and vegetables may or may not be included.

The cottage-garden look

A cottage garden should look good from spring through to autumn and be jam-packed with fragrant plants. The colour scheme should be soft and harmonious – soft purples, blues and pinks – and height is created by growing climbers, such as roses and clematis, up obelisks and posts and allowing them to scramble up trees and along walls. The sensation of being fully enclosed by flowers and their scent adds to the romantic feel.

To create a relaxed feel it's best to plant in swathes (see page 58), interspersing naturalistic-looking grasses with flowers to form a dotty, hazy effect. Repeat planting throughout the garden will provide a little structure to what is typically a very informal look and will create a sense of unity in the design – although a haphazard look is part of the charm of a cottage garden, you don't want it to be entirely formless. You can also use colour to link the different areas together.

Cottage garden beds can be any shape. However, they do need to be of a reasonable size to accommodate enough plants. Having lots of plants is important for this style – allow them to spill onto paths and lawns for a generous, hazy feel.

Maintenance

Throughout this chapter, you'll see this symbol. It indicates the maintenance advice for each plant.

The practicalities

Cottage-garden borders need to be in an open area of the garden that receives sun for most of the day. The soil must be well drained (clay soil does not suit cottage-garden plants). Since there are lots of flowers, it's important to add plenty of organic matter before planting to enrich the soil.

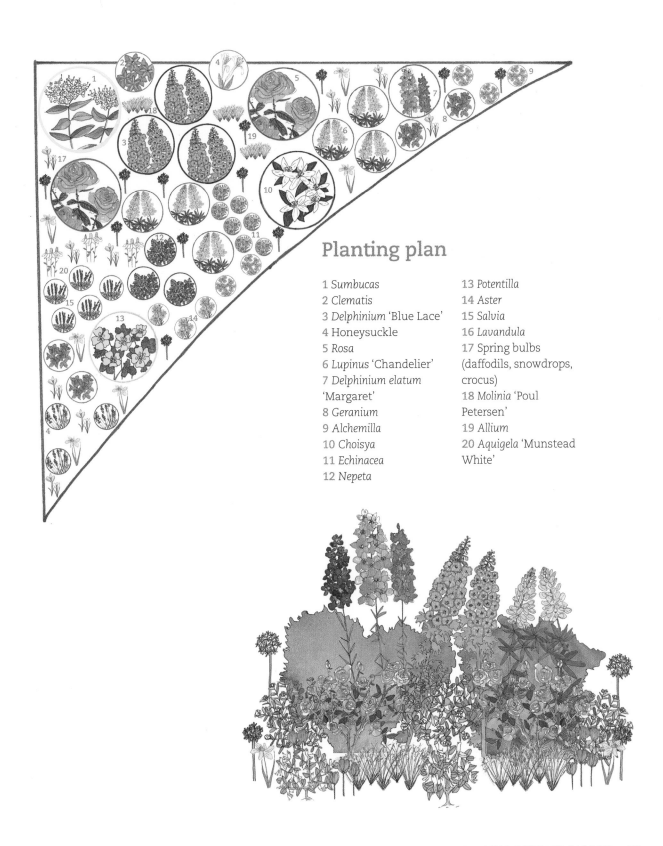

Planting plan

1 *Sumbucas*
2 *Clematis*
3 *Delphinium* 'Blue Lace'
4 Honeysuckle
5 *Rosa*
6 *Lupinus* 'Chandelier'
7 *Delphinium elatum* 'Margaret'
8 *Geranium*
9 *Alchemilla*
10 *Choisya*
11 *Echinacea*
12 *Nepeta*
13 *Potentilla*
14 *Aster*
15 *Salvia*
16 *Lavandula*
17 Spring bulbs (daffodils, snowdrops, crocus)
18 *Molinia* 'Poul Petersen'
19 *Allium*
20 *Aquigela* 'Munstead White'

What to plant

Allium

There are many different forms of alliums. *Allium* 'Ambassador' and *A. hollandicum* 'Purple Sensation' look wonderful planted in groups down the length of a border; they can be woven like a ribbon among other plants and their foliage takes up little room. They have tall slender stems and a sphere of tiny purple flowers at the top. Plant these bulbs with tulips for a magnificent late-spring display. *Allium sphaerocephalon* is also worth considering if you want to experiment with different allium flower forms. It is smaller and has more of a conical shaped flower. It is also a much deeper colour.

Once the flowers have finished leave the foliage alone for at least six weeks, then cut it back to the ground. The bulbs will stay dormant underground until the following year. If you want to move any bulbs or divide clumps into smaller ones and replant them elsewhere in the garden, do this after flowering and when the foliage is starting to go yellow.

Alchemilla mollis (lady's mantle)

A great ground-cover perennial with scalloped foliage and frothy sprays of tiny green flowers in summer, which are good for blending areas together as well as suppressing weeds. Droplets of rain collect on the leaves resembling pearls of liquid mercury.

Alchemilla can self-seed like crazy, so once the flowers start to look tired and tatty remove the stem right to the base of the plant.

Aquilegia vulgaris (columbine)

This is a classic cottage-garden perennial that manages to seed itself in the most unexpected places, sometimes with great results – although you may have to pull out the ones you don't want. It has a lovely informal quality and is a good filler from early spring to early summer. Its foliage is nice and low, leaving its slender stems to grow through other planting. *Aquilegia vulgaris* 'Nivea' is a good choice.

To stop it taking over your plot, remove the flowerheads after flowering. Cut back to the ground when the foliage starts to look tatty.

Aster

Most asters bloom profusely towards the end of summer, with masses of tiny daisy-like flowers in strong mounding shapes. I like to put these perennials towards the front of borders, where they can be enjoyed as other plants are 'quietening down' for the autumn. They are an invaluable source of late nectar for visiting bees and insects. Varieties such as Aster × frikartii 'Mönch' are more resistant to powdery mildew. I also like Aster × frikartii 'Flora's Delight'.

Asters don't like to dry out too much early in the year as it makes them susceptible to powdery mildew, so water regularly until they have plenty of foliage. Cut the whole plant down to the ground in late autumn or spring.

Doris Cottage

Clematis viticella

This is the easiest group of clematis to grow, averaging 2.5–3m in height and with a large range of flower shapes. You are sure to find one you love. When planting clematis, always plant a few inches deeper than it was in the original pot. Planting another plant around the base is beneficial as clematis enjoy shade around their roots. They will need some tying in to trellis or other support initially, but eventually they will wind themselves around it.

Cut the whole plant back to a few inches in spring, removing all the growth except for a pair of buds at the bottom of the stem.

Delphinium

These summer-flowering perennials, which range in colour from white to intense blue, add height and drama to a border. Their huge spires of flowers can reach 2m in some cases. Plant strong plants around them to give support and conceal some of the foliage, which can look untidy very quickly. 'Blue Lace' and 'Margaret' are both good varieties.

Need staking early in the season to support the large flowerheads. Feed every few weeks with a liquid feed in summer and remove any dead flower spikes to encourage side shoots. Cut back to the ground in autumn when the foliage withers.

Best bulbs for cottage gardens

Crocus, Galanthus (snowdrop) and Narcissus (daffodil) bring much-needed spring colour after the bleak winter months. I plant smaller varieties, as I don't like the bulky foliage left by larger ones. I often plant under deciduous shrubs and along the path leading up to the house to provide a cheery welcome.

Echinacea (coneflower)

A wonderful plant which makes a great impact when planted in swathes (see page 58). It has a large daisy-type flower and flowers from late summer into early autumn. Some reliable varieties are 'Magnus' and 'Pink Glow'. They also have fantastic architectural seedheads.

Protect from slugs. This must be done in early spring, because as soon as the new shoots start to emerge the slugs will find them. Once the plant has a good amount of growth the slugs tend to leave it alone – it's the young growth they like. So whatever your method, use it and be vigilant. I like to leave the seedheads on all winter as they have lovely structure. You can then cut the plant back to the ground in spring.

Geranium (cranesbill)

The majority of hardy geraniums are brilliant! There is a hardy geranium for any site and situation. They come in a huge array of heights and colours and do a great job at softening edges of borders and blending areas of planting together. They are also fantastic at providing ground cover and flower for months. One of my favourites is *Geranium* 'Mavis Simpson'. Its tight, low foliage is wonderful for ground cover, it flowers relentlessly and is a gorgeous shade of pink which ties in wonderfully with the colours of a cottage garden. *Geranium himalayense* 'Gravetye' is another great variety, it's a little taller but has deeply cut foliage and a lovely open-faced blue flower.

Cut back to the ground after the first flush of flowers – this is usually early summer. Within a fortnight they will have fresh new foliage and a second flush of flowers that will keep coming until the end of summer through to early autumn. Cut back dead and slimy foliage in autumn. Whatever is left behind needs removing in spring, when the whole plant can be chopped back to ground level.

Fruit trees

Trees in a cottage garden are usually productive, so pick something you would like to eat – apple, pear, damson, plum or cherry are all great choices. Should you want something for a small space, choose a variety on a dwarf rootstock. Fruit trees will all give you blossom as well as fruit, and with a little bit of luck and the right varieties, like *Malus domestica* 'Sunset' or *Malus domestica* 'Fiesta', you should get some fantastic autumn colour, too.

Lavandula (lavender)

A cottage-garden staple, lavender is a must-have plant. It thrives on poor, free-draining soil and loves a bit of neglect, which makes it pretty low maintenance. Once established, you rarely need to water it. Lavender will not tolerate heavy clay and will benefit from some grit being added to the planting hole. It will flower during the summer months and into early autumn, filling your garden with delicious fragrance. 'Hidcote' is a good variety for this type of garden.

 I leave the flowerheads on all winter, as I believe that in colder regions it helps protect the plants from frost. In spring, cut the plant back, removing all the old seedheads. You can be tough and cut back hard, just always leave the stems with some greenery on them. Cutting all the way back into the brown wood will weaken the plant and it may not grow back.

Lonicera japonica var. repens (Japanese honeysuckle)

A gorgeous climber with a heady fragrance. It has long, tubular flowers which appear in small clusters in summer, and twining stems which wrap themselves around anything they can get hold of. Make sure it has something solid to climb up.

 No regular pruning is needed – just tie in the new growth. Remove any dead growth and cut back any long, whippy shoots that you don't need. If you've inherited a mature specimen that needs some rejuvenation, cut the whole plant back to around 60cm in winter or early spring.

Lupinus (lupin)

Lupins come in a huge array of colours, so choose one that suits your scheme. They create wonderful clumps of tall spires and will tolerate dappled shade. Use several times in a border to give a sense of rhythm. They look best in early summer. *Lupinus* 'Chandelier' is a great variety.

 Dead-head to give a second flush of flowers. They may also need protecting from slugs.

Molinia (moor grass)

A native moor grass, *Molinia* will tolerate a range of conditions. The varieties have plumes, some of which are deep purple, while others have more of a golden tone. They also come in several heights meaning it is easy to find one you love.

 The only maintenance required is to cut the whole plant back to a few inches in spring. Easy!

Nepeta (catmint)

Catmint loves a sunny position and free-draining soil and will reward you with clouds of blue flowers from early summer right into the autumn. It also makes good ground cover when planted in groups, which helps to supress weeds, and its domed shape makes a valuable addition to the border. It's a great plant for pollinating insects, too. Cats love the stuff, so if you have a feline friend go for *Nepeta × faassenii* 'Junior Walker', as they seem to be able to resist the urge of rolling around and eating this one. *Nepeta racemosa* 'Walker's Low' is also great for a cottage garden.

🪣 Cut back after its first flush of flowers to encourage more flowers. If it is looking tatty and has lots of slimy dead foliage, cut back to the ground in autumn. Leaving it until spring just leaves a cosy place for snails to hibernate over winter.

Other plants for a cottage garden

- ✤ *Choisya ternata* 'Sundance'
- ✤ *Lonicera japonica* 'Halliana'
- ✤ *Potentilla fruticosa* 'Elizabeth'
- ✤ *Sambucus nigra* 'Aurea'

Phlomis tuberosa

A statuesque plant that looks good towards the back of the border, this has whorls of beautiful flowers in late summer and impressive seedheads, which hold their form over winter.

🪣 Remove dead leaves in autumn, then cut back the stems and remove the old foliage in spring.

Stachys byzantina

With its ground-hugging, soft, silvery leaves, this plant is useful for softening border edges and contrasting with other foliage. It likes a well-drained, sunny spot and has erect spires of flowers, which are pale purple in colour.

🪣 Remove any tatty foliage and dead flowers as soon as you see them. If the plant spreads too far, simply dig out the areas where you don't want it.

Rosa (rose)

The varieties are endless, so my advice is to pick one you love. However, I insist it must have fragrance! If you don't have room in the border for as many as you'd like, grow upwards – cover pergolas, grow around door frames, over walls and up posts. There are many specialist rose breeders online where you can buy varieties that have been bred to resist pests and diseases. *Rosa* 'Gertrude Jekyll' is a good variety to choose, as are 'Constance Spry', 'Felicia' and 'Cottage Rose'.

 I prune roses twice a year – once in late autumn, when I take about one third of their growth away (this prevents wind rock). Then, in spring, I prune them by half again.

Salvia

This is one of my favourite plants and every garden that I have designed has included them within the scheme – they are incredibly versatile and long-flowering. Varieties such as *Salvia nemorosa* 'Amethyst' and 'Ostfriesland' will give you colour over a long period over the summer and they are good for the mid-height section of your border as most of them grow to 0.6–1.2m tall. They have a good shape, need no support and the flower spires contrast well with daisy-like shapes. *Salvia × sylvestris* 'Dear Anja' is another fine choice.

 Dead-heading salvias continually over summer will encourage more flowers.

Sambucus (elder)

The elder is often overlooked yet it has lots to offer, especially in a cottage garden. It has light and graceful sprays of tiny cream flowers, which bloom in summer, and the foliage is delicate and either golden or deep plum depending on the variety. It will also produce elderberries, so whether you grow it to harvest its flowers for elderflower cordial or its berries to make jam, or you just like the way it looks, this shrub is a win-win. Varieties 'Black lace' and 'Aurea' will reliably flower and fruit. Remember, the flowers and the berries are the only edible parts of the plant and should never be eaten raw.

 Cut the whole plant back to the base of the main stem in autumn to keep the new growth at a manageable height.

A cutting garden

If you want to grow flowers for cutting and have the space you might want to create a dedicated 'cutting garden'. You can grow the flowers in a similar fashion to vegetables – in long, uniform rows that you can get in between to weed and harvest your crop.

A cutting garden enables you to grow and pick flowers without ruining the look of your borders and to grow flowers that may not suit your border colour schemes. For instance, if you've got a subtle scheme of muted blues, pinks and purples you can plant a riot of hot-coloured flowers in your cutting garden to take indoors. If you have a lot of space, consider having two or more areas for cut flowers, each in a different colour scheme.

If you don't have the room for a dedicated cut-flower border but like the idea of cut flowers, research which flowers make a good bouquet and are long-lasting when cut and incorporate them into your border. The relaxed style of a cottage garden means you are able to harvest flowers for vases with very little disturbance to your borders.

Five tips for cut flowers

1 Cut flowers early in the morning as the flowers will be most sturdy.

2 Feed your plants a high-potassium feed, for instance a tomato feed. This will encourage more flowers.

3 Cut your flowers regularly, as this will encourage more new growth. If you run out of vases around the house, give bunches away to friends and family.

4 To revive cut flowers that look a little droopy, plunge them into hot then ice-cold water to perk them up. (Come to think of it, I suppose that would perk most things up!)

5 Put a teaspoon of sugar and a dash of bleach in the vase. The sugar will give cut flowers a little energy boost and the bleach will prevent bacteria from developing and spoiling your bouquet.

◀ A cutting garden enables you to grow and pick flowers without ruining the look of your borders.

▼ The seedheads of these poppies are fantastic in floral displays.

Good flowers for cutting

- ✿ Achillea
- ✿ Agastache
- ✿ Alchemilla mollis
- ✿ Astilbe
- ✿ Camassia
- ✿ Eryngium
- ✿ Geum (avens)
- ✿ Helenium
- ✿ Papaver somniferum
- ✿ Rosa

Family garden

If you have children who enjoy being outside, making the most of your garden is essential. Whether you have a budding David Attenborough, an enthusiastic footballer or the next up-and-coming Michelin-starred chef, you can incorporate elements into your garden that will engage with their interests as well as creating areas of planting in which you can allow yourself a moment of calm contemplation.

▶ Little ones love bright colours so be bold, pick one and run with the theme.

Dividing areas

Dividing and screening areas using plants helps to give different members of the family their own space while retaining the overall theme of the garden. Grasses, bamboos and hedges will all do this better than using walls or fences, which might make the garden seem disjointed. Plants also provide a softer finish, which is more in keeping with the requirements of a family unit.

▶ Play equipment can be a bit of an eyesore in the garden, so disguise it with screening plants.

A colourful space

I feel the borders in a family garden should be a riot of colour to mirror the vitality and vibrancy of youth. Once you've worked out your site's conditions, don't be precious about what goes where. Pick plants in colours you all like – deciding where to put them can be something you all have a say in, and getting the kids involved might mean they take a little more care when playing Frisbee!

Use herbaceous plants to fill the borders with colour and scent for the summer. Placing scented plants near the path will encourage little ones to stop and sniff. A good framework of evergreen shrubs will provide interest in winter, and grasses that spread and arch will help to unify the borders. They are very forgiving and can unite the most random colour palette.

Child-friendly plants

Children love sowing seeds, and annual meadow flowers are really easy to sow. Lots of annuals give nice, quick results, which is great as children aren't particularly patient. Giving them a small patch of earth to sow can have magical results, and there are lots of varieties you can grow to encourage wildlife. Annuals like California poppies (*Eschscholzia californica*), cornflowers (*Centaurea cyanus*), corn cockles (*Agrostemma githago*) and love-in-a-mist (*Nigella damascena*) will all do well with very little effort and bring many buzzing insects to the borders. Herbs are also great to grow as you can pick them easily and use them in all kinds of recipes. Likewise, try growing some edible flowers – pansies (*Viola*) and nasturtiums (*Tropaeolum*) are great in salads. Lavender (*Lavandula*) flowers are delicious in shortbread biscuits, and violas look super-pretty if frozen in ice cubes.

If your borders are taking a beating from too many home goals, then some tough plants are what you need. A key element for a family garden is kid-proof planting. Lots of the plants listed on pages 84–91 are grown for foliage and are tough; they also tolerate a wide range of conditions.

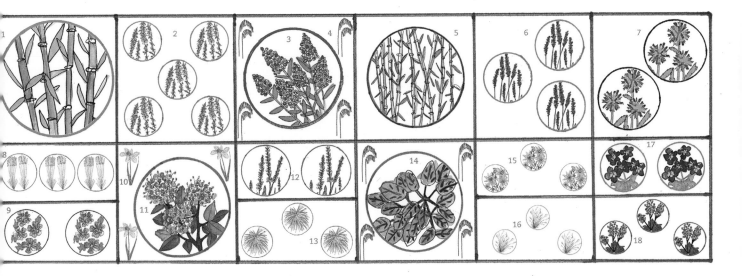

Planting plan

1 *Fargesia* 'Red Panda'
2 *Lythrum Virginatum* 'Dropmore Purple'
3 *Buddleja* 'Lochinch'
4 Bluebells
5 *Fargesia* 'Rufa'
6 *Persicaria Amplexicaulis* 'Firetail'
7 *Echinops Bannaticus* 'Taplow Blue'
8 *Molinia Caerulea* 'Moorhexe'
9 *Geranium Magnificum* 'Rosemoor'
10 Daffodils
11 *Ceanothus* 'Blue Mound'
12 *Persicaria Amplexicaulis* 'Rosea'
13 *Hakonechloa Macra*
14 *Cotinus Coggyrgria* 'Royal Purple'
15 *Astrantia* 'Buckland'
16 *Stipa Tenuissima*
17 *Geranium phaeum*
18 *Huechera* 'Paris'

Beyond the plants

There are endless options and products to encourage your kids to enjoy the garden. With just a little imagination, your garden could be a children's paradise without all the over-sized plastic paraphernalia we end up buying and leaving out all winter to fade and get broken.

Get little ones involved by making fat balls for the birds, planting up a jungle of container plants for their toy dinosaurs, building a den or perhaps something more ambitious, like a tree house. These are sure-fire ways to keep them engaged and entertained while you potter about and carry out your own garden tasks.

If you have any vertical space and your children are of a suitable age, climbing-wall holds are a great addition to a flat surface such as the side of the house and encourage exercise and play while taking up no space. They come in all kinds of colours and shapes and are easy to put up – but of course, supervision is required.

Glow-in-the-dark aggregates and paint are also favourites of mine. How about plastic pebbles that glow in the dark, to lead you along a path or mark out a 'force field' around your den? Painting your prize pots with glow-in-the-dark paint enables you to check on them from your bedroom window at night.

What to plant

Astrantia (masterwort)

These are up there in my list of top five plants. They come in an array of colours ranging from white through to pale pink, deep pink and dark sultry plum shades. They also flower for a long time – if dead-headed, all astrantias can give flowers from early summer until the first frosts of winter, and then they have lovely winter seedheads. *Astrantia* 'Ruby Star' looks fantastic if planted alongside something with lime-green foliage or bracts, and the larger flowers of *A. subsp. involucrata* 'Jumble Hole' look effortlessly pretty for months and months. Astrantias prefer their soil on the damp side, but are tolerant of other conditions if given a good mulch every spring.

Cut back after the first flush of flowers to encourage new growth, and keep dead-heading to encourage more flowers. They should flower again and look good until autumn. In spring, mulch and remove all dead foliage.

Buddleja (buddleia, butterfly bush)

These are must-have shrubs in the family garden. They have long spires of flowers and over 18 species of butterfly enjoy feeding from them. I would stick to planting the purple and blue varieties like 'Black Knight' and 'Lochinch'. The white-flowering ones don't look as attractive when they have finished flowering.

Dead-head regularly before they have a chance to drop their seeds everywhere. I also suggest you prune them down to about 30cm at the end of autumn so the following summer you'll have the flowers at a height you can enjoy them; the less you cut back, the higher your buddleia will bloom.

Buxus sempervirens (box)

Along with *Ilex crenata* (see page 88), this is a neat, small-leaved evergreen and gives great structure. You can trim and shape it into anything you like. Having some solid domes of evergreen throughout the space will really pull everything else together. Buying bare-rooted plants in autumn or winter will save you money, especially if you're planning on planting a lot of them. In recent years, box has been prone to a disease called box blight, which kills the plant very quickly. You shouldn't plant another box in the same spot for several years.

Box can be a hungry plant. Adding compost or manure to its planting hole will give it a good start, and it benefits from a mulch of homemade compost or manure in spring. A liquid feed, such as seaweed, gives it an extra boost in summer. It is grown for its foliage, so go for a feed that has a high nitrogen content. You can trim it twice a year – in early summer a light trim will encourage lots of side shoots, to create a bushy, dense plant. A second trim in late autumn will tidy it up over winter.

Choisya ternata (Mexican orange blossom)

This evergreen shrub has pretty, strongly scented, star-shaped white flowers. Using this alongside other evergreen shrubs will extend the level of interest over the year. It prefers a well-drained spot with lots of sun.

Needs no pruning unless it really gets too big for its space. If that's the case, trim it immediately after it has finished flowering.

Ceanothus (California lilac)

◄ This shrub comes in a large range of sizes, so make sure you check the label before you buy. They have compact, shiny green leaves and blue, fluffy-looking flowers. I like to use the shorter, mounding varieties like *Ceanothus* 'Blue Mound': they stay compact and will give you a cloud of blue flowers to enjoy in spring.

No pruning required if an evergreen variety. If it's a spring/early summer flowering shrub and you think it needs trimming, do this immediately after it has finished flowering. If your variety flowers during the summer, trim by one third to a half in spring.

Cotinus coggygria 'Royal Purple'

I adore this shrub – it has such a fantastic plum-coloured foliage and the way the sun shines through the new growth is delightful. It has large, oval-shaped leaves and, if left to grow, will become a large, rounded shrub. Ideally, position the plant where it can be back lit. It can get big, but correct pruning will keep its size in check.

💧 I cut mine at home back to the base of the main stems; it seems brutal, but pruning like this every autumn keeps its leaves small and its size neat.

Echinops (globe thistle)

Tall and statuesque with a solid stem, these look great at the back of the border. Their blue spherical thistle-like flowers appear in both summer and autumn and will bring in a wealth of pollinating insects – bees love this plant. *Echinops* are very architectural and give great structure. They can get big, so allow plenty of room.

💧 Provides great winter seedheads for the birds. Cut back the whole plant to the ground in spring. It may need staking in its first year. Divide every few years if it gets too big for its spot.

Geranium (cranesbill)

◄ See Romantic Cottage Garden, page 74. For a family garden, go for bold blue varieties that will cover your ground such as *Geranium* 'Johnson's Blue', 'Rozanne' and 'Orion'. They will give you continuous colour in summer and bridge areas of planting, softening strong shapes and suppressing weeds. *G. macrorrhizum* will grow just about anywhere. It spreads and will create dense mats of foliage and flowers of around 30cm high. It will also grow happily in dry shade.

Hebe

These come in all different shapes and sizes, from compact varieties of 40 x 40cm to majestic flowering shrubs at over 1.5m tall. Some hebes, such as *Hebe rakaiensis* and *H.* 'Youngii', create low spreading mounds that provide good ground cover and, as evergreens, create interest all year round. Their small spikes of tubular flowers appear in summer and autumn and attract lots of bees and insects. A good plant, which can be used as a 'bumper' at the front of a border.

 Fuss free. Trim only if necessary, immediately after they have finished flowering.

Bamboos

Bamboos are fantastic for screening and hedging. They make a wonderful rustling noise in the wind and add great movement to a garden. Make sure you read the label and choose wisely as some can be pretty thuggish. They will tolerate full sun or dappled shade. Clumping bamboo (*Fargesia*) and running bamboo (*Phyllostachys*) are just two of many different genus of bamboo. Most varieties of these genus are hardy, but make sure you always read the labels and have adequate space for the

variety you choose. *Pseudosasa* is another brilliantly unfussy genus.

 For any type of bamboo, thin out and cut down spent bamboo canes when required, and remove any debris from the base of the plant. They can be lifted and divided in spring. If planting a *Phyllostachys*, line the sides of the planting hole with paving slabs or corrugated iron to contain it or it will spread.

Hyacinthoides non-scripta (English bluebell)

Bluebells like a shady spot, just as they would in the wild, and as they grow over the years they will multiply, creating a carpet of blue.

Do not remove the foliage for six weeks after flowering. If you want to divide and move clumps of bulbs, wait until the foliage has started to go yellow. Only then will the bulb have re-charged and be strong enough to come back and flower the following year.

Ilex crenata (box-leaved holly)

Like *Buxus sempervirens*, this is great for evergreen structure. A member of the holly family, many garden designers have started using this box alternative over the last few years. It can also be shaped and clipped, with some varieties like 'Golden Gem' having a golden foliage colour. It is a tough little evergreen shrub and will tolerate shade.

Tidy up the plant by removing any dead or damaged shoots in spring. If you want to create a formal shape or hedge, clip in late summer and mulch around the base of the plant with compost or manure.

Lythrum virgatum 'Dropmore Purple'

I love the hot pink colour of this plant in summer. It looks particularly good when planted in groups of three or more, and will liven up a solid mass of evergreen if flowering against it. It also has good winter stems, which stay stiff and turn a lovely shade of bronze. It prefers a damp soil, but is very tolerant of other conditions. A good dose of manure or homemade compost put in the planting hole will help get it established.

Cut back all dead foliage in early spring. Lift and divide in autumn or early spring if it becomes too big or congested, and mulch around the crown in spring.

Molinia (moor grass)

See Romantic Cottage Garden, page 88. *Molinia* subsp. *caerulea* 'Poul Petersen' and *M. caerulea* subsp. *arundinacea* 'Transparent' are good choices for a family garden, being very tough and tolerant of most conditions. They have low foliage and wands of grass that will look good from late summer through to mid-winter. 'Transparent' looks good at the back of a border mixed with tall perennial flowers.

Narcissus (daffodil)

Daffodils en masse remind me of Easter school holidays. If you plant them for no other reason but to remind you that it's nearly time for the Easter bunny to visit, it's worth it. Smaller-growing varieties are my preferred option.

 See *Hyacinthoides non-scripta* (page 88).

Persicaria affinis 'Superba'

This groundcover plant will flower for months and months during summer and autumn and tolerate all kinds of conditions. It has low mat-forming foliage and wands of flowers which on the same plant can range from white and pale pink to deep red.

 If it spreads too much, just dig up the bits you don't want. Cutting back all the dead flowerheads in autumn and removing any dead foliage will also tidy it up.

Rudbeckia fulgida var. sullivantii 'Goldsturm'

A bright yellow daisy. When it has finished flowering at the end of autumn, its fantastic seedheads (see picture) will encourage wildlife to visit through the winter.

 Very easy and reliable. Dead-head the first lot of spent flowers, then, once it has sent up replacements, leave these to go to seed. Lift and divide in autumn or spring if the clump ever gets too big.

Persicaria amplexicaulis

A reliable, strong plant with hot-coloured spires of flowers from summer through to autumn, bold foliage and useful height, which is good for the middle of a border, bridging large shrubs and lower herbaceous plants. It needs no support and holds its shape throughout winter. *Persicaria amplexicaulis* 'Rosea' and 'Blackfield' are two great varieties for longevity of flower. They prefer a moist soil but will tolerate drier conditions.

 Leave to stand over winter. In early spring, cut back all foliage to the ground, removing all dead foliage to make way for new growth coming through, and mulch around the crown. Divide in autumn if it outgrows its spot, or if you'd like another clump elsewhere.

Tulipa (tulip)

Planting tulips in pots is an easy job to do with your children in autumn, no matter what age they are. Pack your pot full, in any colour combinations you like. As far as tulips are concerned, anything goes in my book. I personally love pots of clashing colours, with purple and oranges being my favorite combo. Some tulips are lily flowered and have lovely shaped petals; others, like parrot tulips, have delicate serrated petals that have lots of texture. Mixing these different types of tulips with a range of colours will give your tulip planting a real 'wow' factor.

 See *Hyacinthoides non-scripta* (page 88).

Stipa (feather grass)

There are many different varieties to choose from, and it will depend on where you want to plant it. Some are 1.5m statement plants that look great planted in gravel, others are smaller and will be perfectly happy growing in a pot. They all enjoy the sun and well-drained soil and will give you months of enjoyment. For a family garden, I recommend *Stipa tenuissima* (feather grass), a fantastic grass that sways in the breeze and looks good threaded throughout a border, linking areas together. It's also extremely tactile; you can't help but run your hand through it.

Remove any broken flower stems when you need to, otherwise wait until spring to remove any dead foliage and pull out some of the old plumes to encourage new growth. Just running your hand through the plant and pulling gently should do the trick. Leave any division you want to do until spring. Should the plant have really suffered during the winter, then you can cut the whole thing back to just a few inches in the spring – this should rejuvenate it.

Other plants for a family garden

- ⊛ Astrantia 'Buckland'
- ⊛ Buddleja 'Lochinch'
- ⊛ Echinops bannaticus 'Taplow Blue'
- ⊛ Fargesia 'Jiu'
- ⊛ Fargesia rufa
- ⊛ Geranium × magnificum 'Rosemoor'
- ⊛ Geranium phaeum
- ⊛ Hakonechloa macra
- ⊛ Heuchera 'Paris'

Best trees for a family garden

If you have a sizeable back garden, the willow *Salix alba* 'Tristis' can be a wonderful addition to a family garden. I remember building dens under the canopy of the one we had when I was a child. It likes moisture and grows quickly, so be sure you have the space required – it's a huge tree and can reach 12m in height! The katsura tree (*Cercidiphyllum japonicum*) is smaller and a more sensible choice – but you can't build a den under it! Its leaves are heart shaped and in autumn not only does it go incredible shades of orange and red, it fills the air with an amazing fragrance reminiscent of cinder toffee.

Then there is the good old apple tree (*Malus*). If you have space for only one apple, make sure you choose a self-fertile variety – this will ensure your success at getting some fruit. 'Sunset', 'Ellison's Orange' and 'Spartan' are all good choices. Apple trees are excellent to climb when mature, plus make for a healthy snack dispenser in late summer and have pretty blossom in the spring.

◀ *Cercidiphyllum japonicum.*

Formal garden

Originating from some of the grandest homes in France, the formal garden represents order and harmony. This style of garden uses symmetry and clean lines, and planting consists mainly of evergreen shrubs laid out in a geometric pattern. Most shrubs are neatly clipped and hedging is often shaped. Since a formal garden relies on a strong backdrop of evergreen plants and few flowers, it will look the same for most of the year.

Formal gardens can look very traditional or very modern. The hard landscaping you choose will give your planting scheme a very different feel, as will the geometric shapes you decide to incorporate. For example, using dressed natural sandstone with its smooth, crisp finish will make a garden look and feel much more modern than using randomly cut and very natural materials like riven York stone. The same applies when it comes to geometric shapes, simplicity will look more contemporary than intricate and fussy shapes.

Garden features

One of the main features of this type of garden are focal points, usually placed at the end of a path or at a central axis point in the garden. These draw the eye and create 'pause points' where you can stop and enjoy the garden scene. Water and fountains are often included in a formal garden to create a sense of movement and sound, preventing it from feeling static. Parterres, or knot gardens, are typical too – low and intricate, they are meant to look like an opulent tapestry, with bodies of still water sometimes acting like mirrors, reflecting the symmetrical planting surrounding it. Containers are often placed symmetrically on either side of a door.

Conditions and maintenance

Since a formal garden is mostly made up of evergreens it can cope with some shade. However, they are usually hungry plants, so an annual feed with pelleted chicken manure or a fertiliser with high nitrogen content will keep them looking tip-top. A loamy soil would be ideal, as it is fertile yet free draining.

A formal garden looks best when it is well looked after and neat, so if you're considering this style you'll need to think about whether you can maintain the look. If you feel having an entirely formal garden would be too much work, bear in mind you can take design elements from this style and incorporate them into a more relaxed, informal garden – they will give your garden character and it will matter less if it looks a little rough around the edges.

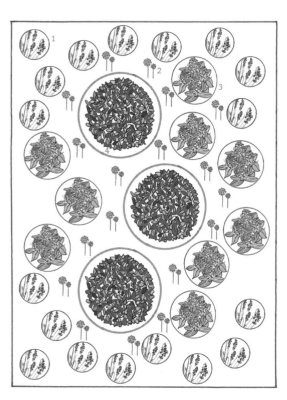

Planting plan

1 *Lavandula*
2 *Allium*
3 *Hebe*
4 *Buxus*

What to plant

Allium

These bulbs will work well in this scheme, especially combined with tulips, and sticking to three colours maximum will give the best effect. Planting in pots and placing them in position while they are in flower, then removing them once they have finished, will also allow you to keep that overall neat and well-maintained finish. *Allium* 'Purple Sensation' is a reliable choice here; their pompom flowerheads add fun to a formal border when planted in groups. For more on Alliums, see Romantic Cottage Garden, page 72.

Buxus sempervirens

See Family Garden, page 85.

Hebe

See Family Garden, page 87. For a formal garden, I would stick with the low-growing evergreen varieties such as 'Caledonia' or 'Red Edge'. Both have a purple tinge to their leaves, which would pick up and enhance any purple flowers such as lavender. Some have a more steely grey-blue tone to them, which would look good with a minimal colour scheme.

Ilex crenata (box-leaved holly)

See Family Garden, page 88.

Lavandula angustifolia 'Hidcote' (lavender)

This lavender is neat and compact, perfect for low hedging. It is also long flowering providing blooms all summer. It needs a sunny position and looks good with other purple flowers of contrasting shape and form.

 See *Lavandula*, Romantic Cottage Garden, page 88.

Herbs

Rosemary, sage and bay are often used in formal schemes – they are all evergreen and like a sunny, well-drained spot. Like any shrub they need a tidy in spring – remove any dead and damaged shoots – but they're otherwise generally low maintenance.

Thuja occidentalis (white cedar)

Statuesque and slender, this is a great evergreen tree that will bring height to a formal garden. Try using several throughout a border in even numbers and mirroring the display on the other side of the garden. If you can only accommodate one, use it as a focal point to lead the eye towards something beautiful or away from something you would rather not have to look at. It can also be useful when planted as a screen to divide up areas of a garden, or to disguise an area such as the bins or a shed.

 Grow in sun and well-drained soil. No pruning required.

Rosa (rose)

These are often used in formal gardens and planted in blocks of the same variety to give solid blocks of colour when in flower. It's best to use varieties that stay relatively small in height and have an upright form. I like *Rosa* 'Munstead Wood' and R. 'Darcey Bussell'. These are compact, so won't impede on each other when grown together and will give you lots of flowers as well as delicious scent.

 See Romantic Cottage Garden, page 77.

Lonicera nitida

▶ Another small-leaved evergreen shrub that is happy to be clipped. The more you clip, the denser it will become, giving you nice tight shapes and straight edges. If you want to enjoy this honeysuckle as a shrub in its natural form, trim it immediately after flowering to control its size.

 Mulch in spring and trim when required. You can trim it at almost any time of year, except on an extremely cold winter's day.

Tulipa (tulip)

As mentioned on page 95, tulips will work well with alliums in this scheme. For more on tulips, see Family Garden, page 90.

See *Hyacinthoides non-scripta* (page 88).

Mediterranean garden

This section could also be called Coastal Garden or Gravel Garden, as all three styles are very closely linked. What they have in common is the plants used in these schemes like lots of sun and well-drained soil. Planting groups of plants that all like the same kind of conditions will instantly make sense when you see them grouped together. Many plants that like these conditions often have silvery or hairy foliage and are frequently highly fragrant, being full of essential oils. A lot of the plants mentioned here can self-seed in the shallowest of soils as they have learnt to adapt to the harsh conditions of being exposed to wind, sun and little water.

Plants and planting

Take inspiration from summer holidays and the beautiful gardens of France, Spain and Italy. To achieve the look, combine relaxed materials like gravel, reclaimed wood and terracotta, and plant formal accents such as cypresses (*Cupressus*) and olives (*Olea*). Terracotta pots are a must, as are lavender (*Lavandula*) and thyme (*Thymus*). Scent will be heavy in the air from pots of herbs and pelargoniums will add pops of vivid colour.

When it comes to placing plants, planting in small groups and leaving lots of open gravel spaces gives a great effect. Don't be afraid to use the odd taller plant among a grouping of small plants – you want it to have a

▲ Gravel is used as a mulch to add to the overall effect.

▶ Terracotta pots are a must for a Mediterannean garden.

slightly rustic charm, and placing your plants in perfect descending order of height will not achieve this. Neither will having everything butting up to each other. Leaving space for plants to scramble and spread will enhance and add to the relaxed theme.

Using gravel

Gravel is often used as hard landscaping in this style of garden. Mediterranean plants dislike having 'wet feet', so a good mulch of gravel will help excess water from sitting around their base.

Gravel gardens work really well in a small front garden. If you have a gravel driveway, too, it creates a nice transition and blurs the lines of where the drive starts and where the garden finishes. This will make the front of your property feel instantly larger and less segmented.

Planting in gravel is simple. You just plant as normal into the soil, but leave the plants slightly protruding from their planting hole, you then mulch thickly with gravel up to the base of the plant. You can use weed membrane under the gravel if you wish, but I think this stops things self-seeding, which is really part of having a gravel garden, and also the gravel tends to move on the membrane a lot. However if weed membrane is going to mean you enjoy your garden more, then use it!

▲ **This** *Gladiolus italicus* **looks great growing out of gravel.**

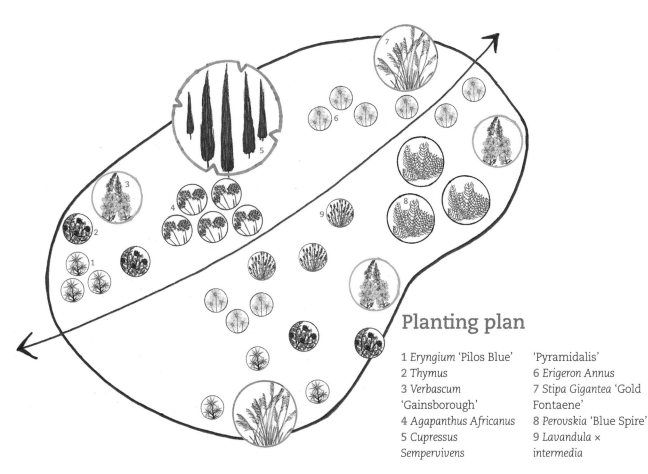

Planting plan

1 *Eryngium* 'Pilos Blue'
2 *Thymus*
3 *Verbascum* 'Gainsborough'
4 *Agapanthus Africanus*
5 *Cupressus Sempervivens*
'Pyramidalis'
6 *Erigeron Annus*
7 *Stipa Gigantea* 'Gold Fontaene'
8 *Perovskia* 'Blue Spire'
9 *Lavandula* × *intermedia*

Achillea (yarrow)

With their flat plates of colour, ranging from pink, to yellow, to red, achilleas are wonderful at providing contrast in shape with other plants, particularly those with a vertical form. The foliage can look tatty while the flowers are still in full swing in summer, so planting a lower-growing plant around achilleas will help to disguise the leaves. Achilleas look especially good as they die, taking on a bronze tone that throughout autumn works brilliantly with the colours of the season. I like using *Achillea* 'Coronation Gold' and 'Moonshine'.

Cut back to the ground in spring to make way for all the new growth. A good mulch around the crown at the same time will also be beneficial.

What to plant

Agapanthus (African lily)

These beautiful plants have vibrant green stems and flowers that resemble exploding fireworks in mid-summer through to early autumn. They come in a variety of stunning blues as well as white. The foliage stays low so they're effective running through a scheme, and they also look great in a pot.

Agapanthus love to have their roots restricted and enjoy sharp drainage. Planting them close to each other helps them thrive. A few handfuls of grit in their planting hole will work wonders. If it gets below -5°C over winter, I would peg some fleece over their crowns or cover them with a thick mulch.

Anthemis

Anthemis has gorgeous white or yellow daisy-like flowers from mid- to late summer and grows to about 70cm. Its egg-yolk centre contrasts brilliantly with lavender.

They can wilt slightly on an overcast day, but don't be tempted to dead-head them as they will sit back up when the sun comes out. Wait until they have started to go brown before cutting the stem back and dead-heading.

Crambe cordifolia

A striking plant with impressive branches of tiny white flowers that reach up to 2m. Although a large display is given, the foliage stays low and its flowers give a lovely hazy cloud-like appearance. It's easier to place at the back of the border, but if you are feeling brave put it towards the front – it might not work, but it will be exciting, and you can always move it in the autumn. It likes a fertile, well-drained soil and will tolerate partial shade. Plant with grasses to great effect.

 Cut down to the ground in autumn.

Erigeron annuus

A delicate plant that produces white daisies right from early summer and into mid-autumn. It will grow and self-seed almost anywhere, making it perfect for gravel.

 Cut back in autumn or spring. Any plants that have self-seeded in gravel where you don't want them are easy to pull out.

Cupressus sempervirens (Italian cypress)

Slender and tall, this evergreen conifer evokes visions of Tuscan hills and, if planted throughout a garden, can create a wonderful impact and unify the space; it really sets the tone for the Mediterranean theme. It requires moist but well-drained soil initially but will tolerate drier conditions once established.

No need to prune, but if your garden is exposed to harsh winds plant in your most sheltered spot.

Dove Cottage

Eryngium (sea holly)

These can be quite tricky to place and the varieties are very different in form and size. I find the easiest ones to work with are *Eryngium bourgatii* 'Picos Blue' and *Eryngium × zabelii* 'Big Blue'. The blue thistle form gives lots of interest and is particularly effective in a gravel garden. The seedheads are just as beautiful. Growing plants that scramble around their base will soften the look and integrate them into the surrounding planting scheme.

They must have good drainage, so adding grit to the planting hole and mulching around the plant with gravel will help it thrive. Cut back to the ground in spring.

Lavandula × intermedia

This lavender works well in this style of garden as it has a more relaxed and graceful form than many other lavenders, such as *L. angustifolia* cultivars, which are more formal and compact.

 See *Lavandula*, Romantic Cottage Garden, page 75.

Lilium (lily)

Lilies bring an exotic look to any planting scheme. I enjoy using the Oriental and the Asiatic lilies in pinks, plums and whites. Growing them in containers means you can place them anywhere in the garden when they look their best and take them indoors in the winter if necessary. Plant them in autumn for summer displays.

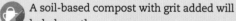 A soil-based compost with grit added will help keep the planting medium moist yet well drained. Replace the top 5cm of compost with fresh compost every spring. If you have harsh winters, taking the pots inside to a frost-free garage or shed will help protect them.

Nerine bowdenii

Extremely glamorous, this shocking-pink umbel is a real head-turner. It likes a sheltered position with full sun and flowers in late summer to early autumn. Planting it en masse along a bank can look spectacular if you have the space.

 In cold areas, protect with a deep mulch.

Olea (olive)

Mature olive trees can be a little pricey but make a true specimen plant. They have trunks full of gnarly character and lovely glaucous-blue foliage. An olive tree looks spectacular if underplanted with lavender.

If you have winters with temperatures as low as -10°C, bring them indoors. This is easier if they're grown in a container. Keep the soil moist over summer and feed monthly whilst in this growing season. Reduce watering in winter, but don't allow the soil to dry out completely. Don't start feeding again till late spring with a liquid fertiliser.

Origanum vulgare '*Compactum*' (marjoram)

I often grow this more for its shape and flower than its culinary uses. It has a lovely small domed habit and the purple flowers during summer attract a wealth of pollinating insects. I like to place it at the edge of a border where it can spill onto a path or in the top of a wall where it will tumble down.

Cut back to the ground at the end of autumn if the foliage has become slimy, otherwise leave until spring.

Pelargonium

Pelargoniums have beautiful flowers and come in colours that, en masse, remind me of a sweet shop. Their foliage is deliciously perfumed. They look magical in terracotta pots, placed on a series of steps, adorning a windowsill or as a centrepiece on a garden table. An essential for a Mediterranean garden.

Water throughout summer to prevent the soil from drying out and feed fortnightly with tomato fertiliser to encourage flowers. If you want to keep them until the following year take them indoors over winter. Trim off any dead leaves and remove any growth that distracts from the shape you want. Allow the soil to fully dry out between watering in the winter months.

Palms

A Mediterranean-style garden without a palm of some kind will always look like it's missing something. Many palms are hardy, and they love lots of sun and free-draining soil. My favourites are the Chusan palm (*Trachycarpus fortunei*) and dwarf fan palm (*Chamaerops humilis*). Placing them as a focal point can be effective, as using other architectural foliaged plants around them will create an exotic feel for your border. Both of these plants are low maintenance except in winter, when you might want to protect them by strapping the leaves up and covering them in horticultural fleece (see page 155).

Perouskia

A member of the sage family, this shrub has pretty spires of blue flowers from mid-summer well into autumn on upright, stiff stems and scented foliage. It looks its best when planted in groups of three or more and likes lots of sun. If left to stand over winter, its stems go white and have a lovely ethereal quality to them – leave them on the plant so you can enjoy them.

Cut back all the stems to at least 5cm in spring.

Salvia

See Romantic Cottage Garden, page 77. Whether they're planted among grasses, next to *Achillea*, or nestled between rosemary and thyme, a salvia will always look fantastic in a Mediterranean Garden.

Rosmarinus officinalis (rosemary)

A small evergreen shrub with pretty blue flowers. Varieties such as *Rosmarinus officinalis* 'Miss Jessopp's Upright' are more upright in form and can look brilliant as a small hedge. Others, such as Prostratus Group are mat-forming and will give you fantastic ground cover. Great in containers as well as in borders, rosemary is perfect in this style of garden.

Likes poor, well-drained soil so don't over-feed or mulch. Needs very little trimming unless it suffers damage over winter, in which case remove the stems that look dead or damaged in spring.

Solanum crispum 'Glasnevin'

This is a semi-evergreen climber full of tiny purple, star-shaped flowers during summer and autumn that give off a lovely fragrance. It likes moist but well-drained soil. Adding homemade compost or leaf mould to the planting hole will help it hold on to some moisture.

No need to trim unless it starts growing where you don't want it to, in which case prune after flowering. Ideally, mulch in spring.

Stipa

See Family Garden, page 90. Both golden oat (*Stipa gigantea*) and feather grass (*Stipa tenuissima*) are brilliant additions to a Mediterranean garden. Both have very different forms but act like a glue that will bring your planting scheme together by adding movement and texture. Plant in well-drained soil in a sunny site.

Other plants for a Mediterranean garden

- *Cupressus sempervirens* 'Pyramidalis'
- *Stipa gigantea* 'Gold Fontaene'
- *Verbascum chaixii* 'Gainsborough'

Thymus vulgaris (thyme)

There are many varieties of thyme and in this style of garden you can never have too many. They look great tucked into cracks in paving, planted in pots or just left to spread and find their way in a patch of gravel. Some are very low-growing and create mats of tiny purple flowers in late spring to early summer, which, when stepped on, release the most fantastic aroma.  **Likes sharp drainage in an open, sunny spot. Cut back in spring to tidy.**

Trachelospermum jasminoides (star jasmine)

This is an excellent climber. Not only does it release a heady, exotic fragrance that fills the air, it is also evergreen. It likes full sun and well-drained soil in a sheltered site. Clusters of star-shaped white flowers in summer are followed by decorative bean-like pods. It will need some form of trellis to climb, and helping it on its way by tying in those early bits of growth will give you greater coverage, quicker.

No need to trim but if you need to restrict its size, prune after flowering, which is usually late summer. Benefits from a good mulch in spring.

Verbascum

I love using these in a Mediterranean garden – the tall, slim spires of yellow or sometimes pale orange draw the eye and puncture the occasional flatness of gravel gardens. They are extremely elegant and look good planted as a single specimen as well as in groups.

Leave the seedheads on over the winter, then in the spring pull the whole plant up. They are usually annuals or biennials, so the seed will grow giving you foliage one year, then flower the following. If left to seed you will seldom go a year without them.

Naturalistic
garden

As a designer living on the cusp of the Yorkshire countryside I aspire to a naturalistic garden as my signature look. It is a style that lends itself perfectly to my surroundings. Naturalistic planting is a very relaxed affair – lots of herbaceous plants are mixed with grasses and planted in drifts and swathes (see page 58), the border edges are blurred and tall plants are woven through smaller ones, resulting in borders that have no real front and back. Curved beds really accentuate this kind of planting.

Naturalistic planting

The plants you grow should encourage plenty of pollinators – bees, butterflies and the many insects that visit will all add to that feeling of the space being naturalistic. Having large clumps of the same plant repeated throughout a border will replicate what you see in nature – if a plant is thriving in its site you will usually see lots of it. To achieve this look, plant in groups and use grasses to soften the bold blocks of plant forms. The right grass can give even the most formal arrangement a naturalistic quality.

Attempting to recreate nature can be far trickier than you may think, and keeping the border interesting all year is really where the skill lies. One of the main attractions (and challenges) of this type of planting is that it should look attractive after everything has finished flowering, so choose plants with a good structure and seedheads that look attractive over winter. They should also be self-supporting, as stakes detract from the look.

◄ Using the borrowed landscape and bringing the surroundings into the garden with planting.
▲ Mirroring colour in different flower forms adds depth.

▲ Allium seedheads are just as valuable aesthetically as when they are in full flower.

Conditions and maintenance

This style of planting has many flowers, so lots of sunshine is important, as is an open spot. Avoid shady sites and planting under trees, as you'll find that the plants will lean in the direction of the sun, which can really spoil the look you're trying to create. A moist but well-drained soil is ideal. However, the plants suggested in the following pages are tough and will tolerate drier conditions provided they're mulched annually in spring.

If the plants are grown in the right conditions, they need little in the way of support or mollycoddling once they are in. Just cut them back once a year.

Planting plan

1 *Thalictrum* 'Elin'
2 *Eupatorium Maculatum* 'Atropurpureum'
3 *Miscanthua sinensis* 'Kaskade'
4 *Eupatorium* 'Purple Bush'
5 *Aruncus* 'Horatio'
6 *Calamygrostis Brachytricha*
7 *Sanguisorba officianalis* 'Arnhem'
8 *Perxicaria Amplexicaulis* 'Blackfield'
9 *Thalictrum* 'Hewitts Double'
10 *Astrantia* 'Florence'
11 *Persicaria bistorta* 'Horte Tarte'
12 *Echinachea purpurea* 'Pink Glow'
13 *Astrantia* 'Superstar'
14 *Aster* 'Coombe Fishacre'
15 *Sedum telephium* 'Karfunkestien'
16 *Persicaria* 'Rosea'
17 *Salvia Nemerosa* 'Carradonna'
18 *Echinacea* 'Prairie Splendour'
19 *Nepetea racemosa* 'Walker's Low'
20 *Geranium* 'Dilys'
21 *Echinacea* 'White Swan'

New Perennial Movement

The naturalistic garden style is sometimes referred to as the New Perennial Movement. New Perennialists, like Piet Oudolf, use a range of herbaceous perennials and grasses planted in drifts to create a naturalistic look. There is huge emphasis on trying to establish a link to nature. Plants are chosen for form and structure and great attention is given to planting the right plant in the right place.

What to plant

Agastache

This is a great plant with tall tufts of flowers. They are usually blue and purple, although there are some orange flowering varieties. They flower from mid-summer all the way into autumn. They look good in large clumps and against a contrasting flower form such as *Echinacea*. *Agastache* 'Blue Fortune' is great.

 Leave the seedheads on over winter. In the spring, cut back and give it a good mulch.

Aruncus 'Horatio'

This is a plant I often overlook. However, while taking photographs for this book at Cow Close in North Yorkshire I saw this plant teamed with a *Sanguisorba* (see pages 108–109 for picture) and it looked fantastic, so I just had to use it in this scheme. It has creamy panicles of tiny flowers in early summer and creates a big clump, so is a great foil for other flowers as well as a solid support.

 In spring, cut back the whole plant to a few inches from the ground.

Aster

No naturalistic border should be without a few of these plants. They are amazing for their vibrant colour when everything else is starting to slow down. They come in a range of heights and varieties, so you really have no excuse for not squeezing them into your scheme. For more on Asters, see Romantic Cottage Garden, page 73.

Maintenance is as on page 73, except that for a naturalistic garden, you should leave on the dead foliage over winter, then trim it all to the ground in spring or before new foliage starts to emerge from the base.

Astrantia (masterwort)

See Family Garden, page 84. *Astrantia* 'Superstar' and *Astrantia major* 'Florence' are two good options for this style of garden.

Calamagrostis brachytricha (diamond grass)

I love this grass – its plumes are foxtail in shape and appear in August, turning a lovely purpley pink, and tall, which is really useful in any scheme. It also looks spectacular when it has rained as the water droplets collect on the plumes and glisten, hence its common name – diamond grass.

🪣 Cut back to the ground in early spring before new growth emerges.

Crataegus laevigata 'Paul's Scarlet'

This is my favourite tree. It has rough bark, early lime-green foliage and tiny clusters of rose-like flowers that remind me of growing up and enjoying the first days of summer when it was warm enough not to have to wear a coat to school. It is native to the UK and, with its unkempt wild appearance and short rounded shape, it is perfect for a naturalistic setting. It will reach a maximum of 4.5m at full maturity.

🪣 None required, but benefits from a mulch around the base.

Dove Cottage

Echinacea pallida (coneflower)

▲ *Echinacea pallida* works really well in this style of planting. Its slender frame has a wild, untamed look that is particularly attractive. It looks good tussling with tall, airy grasses in the breeze.

🪣 Protect from slugs in early spring. Leave the seedheads on over winter and cut the whole plant back to the ground in spring.

Eryngium planum

The blue thistle form of this plant, which flowers from summer into autumn, lends itself brilliantly to this kind of planting scheme. Once mature, its clumps, with their stiff stems and blue seedheads, are sure to grab your attention. It likes sun.

🪣 Cut back to the ground in spring.

Tip
Always try to plant in threes, fives, or sevens if possible, for this scheme especially.

Eupatorium (Joe Pye weed)

◀ Joe Pye weed, as it's commonly known, is a statement plant; growing up to 6ft in one season, this perennial is no shrinking violet. The deep plum stems of *Eupatorium maculatum* Atropurpureum Group are wonderful for planting alongside grasses such as *Miscanthus sinensis* 'Kaskade'. Their contrasting foliage and shapes are harmonised by their purple displays.

🪣 The big stems of this plant are great for sheltering small insects over winter. With this in mind, I would leave it standing until spring, then cut it all the way back to the crown of the plant.

Geranium (cranesbill)

See Romantic Cottage Garden, page 74.

Molinia caerulea subsp. arundinacea 'Transparent'

See *Molinia*, Romantic Cottage Garden, page 75. An extremely elegant grass, this has low foliage and long, slightly arching stems that can be used to create a subtle veil between planting.

Nepeta (catmint)

See Romantic Cottage Garden, page 76. *Nepeta racemosa* 'Walker's Low' is good for this scheme.

Persicaria amplexicaulis

See Family Garden, page 89. *Persicaria amplexicaulis* 'Blackfield' and 'Rosea' would both work well.

Pimpinella major 'Rosea'

Extremely pretty, this pale pink umbellifer (plants with clusters of flowers, looking rather like cow parsley) looks gorgeous either in clumps or weaving its way through other perennials towards the front of a border during early and mid-summer. It does like to self-seed, though, so should you want to limit its ability to end up everywhere, remove its flowerheads before the seeds drop. Don't worry too much if you forget – the seedlings are easy to remove in spring.

 Cut back the whole plant to the ground in spring.

Helenium (sneezeweed)

These look their best when planted in clusters. Varieties such as *Helenium* 'Sahin's Early Flowerer' look great in this style of planting – they have flowers resembling shuttlecocks in shades of warm orange and umber with tall slender stems, flowering at a height of about 1.2m. 'Moerheim Beauty' also looks great – this flowers earlier and the flowers are a deep red. They also make good cut flowers for vases.

These have beautiful seedheads, so leave them on over winter and remove all stems and dead foliage in spring. They may need staking in their first year, but once they have bulked out they should be fine. If planting two clumps in the garden, give one clump the 'Chelsea chop' (see page 154). This will delay flowering by a couple of weeks, giving you a longer stretch of floral interest.

Sanguisorba (burnet)

This is a fun plant, with eccentric tassels and fluffy heads. It has relatively low foliage and stiff, wiry stems. The deep plum-coloured flowerheads of *Sanguisorba* 'Blackthorn' will jangle around with wonderful effect, while the low-growing *Sanguisorba officinalis* 'Red Buttons' has lovely burgundy flowers. *Sanguisorba officinalis* 'Arnhem' is another great choice.

 Remove any broken stems in autumn and cut the rest back in spring.

> ### Tip
> Even if you have decided where you think all your plants are going to go within the bed, don't be shy about experimenting with heights and colour. Before planting, shift them around – it can be fun to see all the different options and you may find one way looks considerably better than another.

Sedum

Sedums are tough, reliable plants. I always 'Chelsea chop' around mid-May (see page 154), otherwise they tend to collapse as they come into flower. *Sedum* (Herbstfreude Group) 'Herbstfreude' ('Autumn Joy') is readily available in most garden centres, but varieties with plum foliage, like *Sedum* 'Matrona' or 'José Aubergine', are worth tracking down if you want something a little more special. *Sedum telephium* 'Karfunkelstein' is another great option.

🖐 Some of the stems will be strong enough to stand over the winter months, but cut back any weak or soggy ones to the base of the plant in autumn. Cut the whole plant back to the ground in spring. Divide any clumps that grow too large in autumn or early spring.

Stipa gigantea (golden oat)

The long, dramatic golden-coloured panicles of this grass look incredible with the late sun on them. They look brilliant if threaded through the back of a border, but are also just as effective on their own, either by a path or as a specimen plant with space to show off.

🖐 Remove any broken or snapped stems when they occur. In spring, running your hand through the foliage and removing tatty or dead foliage will encourage new growth. Divide in spring.

Sorbus 'Joseph Rock'

This is a spectacular tree. With its pinnate leaves, great autumn colour and stunning berries, it would be a valuable addition to any garden. Being a native to the UK, it will flourish there, and is hardy, fuss free and in keeping with the naturalistic theme. It is an upright bushy tree with a mature height of 8–12m.

🖐 None required, although you should remove dead, damaged or diseased growth. It will always benefit from a mulch around the base.

Thalictrum (meadow rue)

This plant is a real showstopper due to its height and delicate flowers. *Thalictrum* 'Elin' grows up to 2.5m and has sprays of white and mauve flowers during the summer. Most thalictrums grow to and above 1.5m high and are invaluable for giving good structure. Their leaves are also among the first to emerge in spring. *Thalictrum delavayi* 'Hewitt's Double' and *Thalictrum* 'Black Stockings' are great examples.

 Cut back to a few inches and divide if necessary in spring.

Other plants for a naturalistic garden

- ❀ *Echinacea purpurea* 'Pink Glow'
- ❀ *Echinacea purpurea* 'Prairie Splendor'
- ❀ *Geranium* 'Dilys'
- ❀ *Miscanthus sinensis* 'Kaskade'
- ❀ *Persicaria bistorta* 'Hohe Tatra'
- ❀ *Salvia nemorosa* 'Caradonna'

Best bulbs for a naturalistic garden

Allium cernuum looks great coming up around the early foliage of perennials such as meadow rue (*Thalictrum*) and grasses such as *Calamagrostis brachytricha*.

Camassia is a wonderful plant. It has stiff green linear leaves and clear racemes that produce a mass of star-shaped blue and violet flowers. It looks particularly attractive set among grasses that are yet to plume.

Sweeping areas of crocus always look good under trees and deciduous shrubs. I like using *Crocus tommasinianus* and *Crocus chrysanthus* var. *fuscotinctus*. These are smaller and more delicate than other varieties opening their beautiful goblet-shaped flowers in spring. Be as generous as you can for real jaw-dropping impact.

Veronicastrum

Tall and slim, these plants have gentle spires of flowers from early summer through to autumn. They come in all different shades of pink as well as white and their leaves whorl around the stem in an attractive way. In the autumn, they can give impressive colour displays – the image here shows a striking yellow autumn plant. For maximum impact, plant them in groups of three or more. Try *Veronicastrum virginicum* 'Erica' alongside *Sanguisorba* 'Blackthorn' for a wonderful contrast in shape and texture.

Cut back all the way to the ground in spring and mulch around the crown at the same time.

Wildlife
garden

▲ Areas of shade are essential for a wildlife garden.

Whether you have room for a wildflower meadow or just three pots of sunflowers, having a garden loved by wildlife will make you enjoy it more too. A little research is required if you want to create a whole garden aimed at wildlife, but the rewards are wonderful.

Wildlife gardens tend to be a bit rough around the edges and the choice of plants is very much led by what they have to offer in terms of shelter and food. The garden needs to be a little untidy and not too well tended – piles of logs and heaps of leaves will have a new appeal once you see what likes to hide among them. A wildlife garden can take time to establish, but once you see the benefits wildlife has on your garden, there will be no turning back.

▶ Leave seed heads in winter to attract wild life year-round.

Habitats and diversity

Water is one of the most important components here – a wildlife pond (see page 168) with an area of bog planting alongside will encourage damp-loving creatures like frogs, toads and newts as well as insects and birds. A border full of bright, nectar-rich flowers will have your garden buzzing with pollinating insects and butterflies, and plants with good seedheads and berries means the birds will come flocking in. The perfect wildlife garden will include a variety of different conditions to attract a diverse selection of creatures to your site. But don't worry if you don't have it all. Wet shade can be created using a pond, trees and shrubs, and planting most flowers in full sun will ensure they are seen by pollinators.

Dove Cottage

Wildlife-friendly plants

Think about the wildlife you want to attract and choose plants accordingly, so you can give the creatures the best deal in town. Shrubs and trees are really important in this type of garden. All wildlife requires shelter and food, and choosing the right shrubs and trees will give you this in abundance.

Many town and inner-city gardens lack roosting and nesting sites, which is why there are not as many birds visiting the garden as there could be. *Sorbus* is one of the trees I use a lot for this very reason, as it's great for providing shelter, nesting material and food. Many varieties are reasonably small so they suit most gardens. Fruit trees are good, too: a crab apple (*Malus sylvestris*) will produce great blossom for insects and fruit for birds and other

Size alert!

Choose trees only that you have room for. You don't want to encourage wildlife to settle then have to remove a tree that gets too big, as this will cause an unnecessary disturbance to your wildlife lodgers.

▲ *Actea* attract wildlife and give a great scent.

creatures later in the year, and one of my all-time favourites is the hawthorn (*Crataegus*) because not only does it provide for the wildlife, I just think the flowers are so pretty. Certain shrubs, including *Cotoneaster*, are loved by bees, so much so that the noise from a mature *Cotoneaster* can be deafening while the bees buzz busily as they collect the pollen.

Climbers are also great for wildlife, and even the smallest garden can accommodate at least one climber. Winter-flowering jasmine (*Jasminum nudiflorum*), honeysuckle (*Lonicera*) and climbing hydrangea (*Hydrangea anomala* subsp. *petiolaris*) are all great for nesting birds and nectar-drinking insects like bees and butterflies. Ivy (*Hedera*) is fantastic for providing late nectar and shelter for many creatures, and mature ivy makes a great nesting site – I have had wrens in mine this year.

Greener gardening

Making your own compost, encouraging wildlife and not using pesticides is a much greener way to garden. It takes dedication and requires patience but over time you will strike a balance in which the wildlife will clean up the pests, the compost will feed the plants and the plants will feed and encourage the wildlife. A beautiful and beneficial circle for all involved.

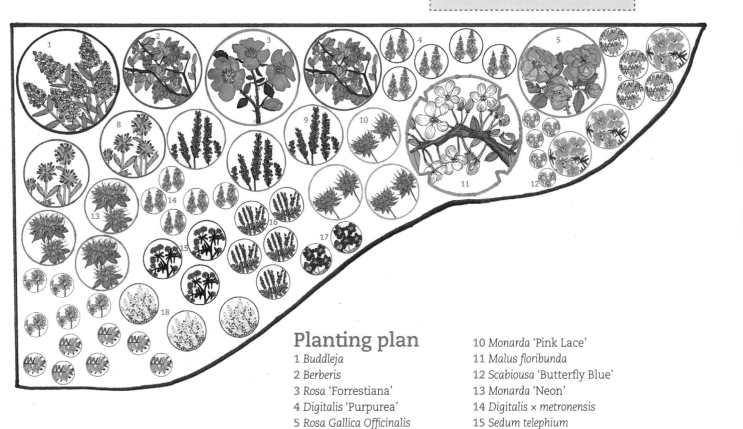

Planting plan

1 *Buddleja*
2 *Berberis*
3 *Rosa* 'Forrestiana'
4 *Digitalis* 'Purpurea'
5 *Rosa Gallica Officinalis*
6 *Erica carnea*
7 *Geranium* 'Elke'
8 *Echinops* 'Veitch's Blue'
9 *Persicaria* 'Fat Domino'
10 *Monarda* 'Pink Lace'
11 *Malus floribunda*
12 *Scabiousa* 'Butterfly Blue'
13 *Monarda* 'Neon'
14 *Digitalis* × *metronensis*
15 *Sedum telephium* 'Karfunkestien'
16 *Salvia* 'Ostfriesland'
17 *Geranium* 'Orion'
18 *Calamintha* 'Nepeta Nepeta'

What to plant

Berberis thunbergii

This is a shrub that is hot on the foliage front! Whether you opt for the sultry plum shades of *Berberis thunbergii* f. *atropurpurea*, the golden glow of *B. thunbergii* 'Aurea' or the in-your-face 'Orange Rocket', you're sure to find one to suit your planting scheme as well as your visiting wildlife's taste buds. They have small leaves and dropping racemes of tiny flowers in spring. The colour of the flowers depends on the variety you pick, as does the mature height and spread, so remember to read the label. Providing flowers, berries and shelter, these shrubs are real 'box-tickers' on the wildlife garden list.

This plant is tough as old boots. Should it get too big for its spot, you can cut it back as hard as you want to – usually after it has finished flowering, but if you want to save berries for wildlife over winter it will cope perfectly well with the same treatment in spring.

Buddleja (buddleia, butterfly bush)

See Family Garden, page 84. You can't really call your garden a wildlife garden without planting a couple of these shrubs, which are really popular with butterflies. *Buddleja davidii* 'Blue Horizon' is good for a wildlife scheme.

Calamintha nepeta subsp. nepeta

This perennial is great positioned towards the front of a border and will give you clouds of tiny mauve flowers that prove to be a magnet for bees in early autumn. Plant in clusters as fillers for impact.

Cut back the whole plant to the base in autumn or spring. I tend to do this in autumn as they have dense dead foliage where snails like to hide.

Dove Cottage

Digitalis (foxglove)

Foxgloves are adored by bees. I have always loved watching bees disappear into their bell-like flowers, often exiting glowing from an all-over covering of golden pollen. Their statuesque spires fail to look anything but impressive wherever they are and seeing them en masse is always a magnificent sight if you can dedicate the space. *Digitalis × mertonensis* and *Digitalis purpurea* both work very well. I like foxgloves in all colours, but pick ones that go with your scheme. They flower in early summer.

These are biennial, so leave the flower to drop its seed in autumn then remove the whole thing in winter or spring. The seed that has dropped will produce foliage in the first year, then flower in the second year.

Cirsium rivulare 'Atropurpureum'

This spectacular burgundy-coloured thistle looks best in summer. It looks good on its own, among other perennials or scattered in a meadow. It has wonderfully attractive foliage and long stems, so I enjoy using it towards the front of borders. Birds love to feast on the seedheads.

Divide any congested mature clumps in autumn or leave seedheads on plants over winter and cut back in spring.

Dipsacus fullonum (teasel)

Teasels are popular with bees and birds – particularly goldfinches, which love their seeds. This native species is a biennial, so if you sow the seeds in spring it will flower the following year. It has erect, spiky foliage, so place away from areas you might brush past. Its tiny blue flowers flower in bands around the flowerhead during the summer months. It has great winter structure and bristly seedheads that look fab in the frost.

🔒 Cut down the seedheads in spring and beware – the teasel can be a prolific self-sower; early management of young seedlings will stop them overtaking the borders.

Echinops (globe thistle)

See Family Garden, page 86. *Echinops ritro* 'Veitch's Blue' is a good choice for a wildlife scheme.

Erica carnea (winter heath)

Heathers have the reputation of being a bit old-fashioned, but I think they are brilliant for many reasons: first, because they remind me of my home in Yorkshire and second because they are great for ground cover and are an invaluable source of nectar for bees and other insects early in the year. They have narrow dark green leaves and erect racemes of tiny urn-shaped flowers during winter and early spring. *Erica carnea* 'Nathalie' and *E.c.* 'Pink Spangles' are good for a wildlife garden.

🔒 You can trim off the dead flowers once they have turned brown, but apart from that they need no other looking after.

Helianthus annuus (sunflower)

The sunflower is a wildlife garden no-brainer. It's wonderful to grow with children and incredibly satisfying if you manage to grow one with height. Lots of modern varieties are shorter and bushier than the species, making them ideal for mixing with perennials in a border. However, they will grow happily in pots should you be short of space. Sunflowers are loved by bees, insects and birds, and flower in early autumn.

🔒 Collect some of the seed for yourself to re-sow the following year.

Lythrum salicaria (purple loosestrife)

The purple loosestrife prefers a damp soil. If you have somewhere suitable, I can highly recommend it. Not only will you be able to enjoy the vivid pink flower spires during the summer, it is also a favourite teatime treat of the elephant hawk moth. Anything that is going to entice these incredible creatures in a garden is worthwhile.

🔒 Cut down to the ground in spring and mulch around the base.

Dove Cottage

Malus sylvestris (crab apple)

This tree produces clusters of flowers in the spring which have white rounded petals flushed with pink. Bees and insects will gorge on them and the fruit in autumn will also entice small mammals such as mice, voles and even foxes. This is a small rounded tree and will grow up to 12m tall.

Needs very little in the way of pruning. However, as with any tree, shrub or plant, always remove what is dead, damaged or diseased.

Monarda (bee balm, bergamot)

▲ These are among my favourite garden plants, not just because of their value in providing nectar and pollen for many pollinating insects, but also because I simply love the way they look – like nothing else. Their shaggy heads of crimson or purple flowers from mid-summer through to mid-autumn never fail to make me smile and the foliage smells incredible! *Monarda didyma* 'Pink Lace' and 'Neon' would both be great for this scheme.

Leave the seedheads on over winter and cut back the whole plant to ground level in spring. Its roots are often close to the surface so water well in dry periods and mulch thickly in spring.

Persicaria amplexicaulis

See Family Garden, page 89. Hoverflies and bees go mad for this plant.

Rosa (rose)

Shrub roses are a great addition to the back of a wildlife garden border, providing shelter and food to many birds. Choosing a single-flowered variety, such as *Rosa* 'Francis E. Lester' or *R. moyesii* 'Geranium', provides easy access for insects to get to the nectar and pollen. British natives, like *R. rugosa* (pictured), can also look fantastic when planted as a hedge and produce the most fantastic jewel-like hips. *R. forrestiana* and *R. gallica* var. *officinalis* are two other great choices.

See Romantic Cottage Garden, page 77.

Salvia

See Romantic Cottage Garden, page 77. For a wildlife garden, I recommend using blue and purple flowering varieties. Blue is the colour that bees can see the most, so this helps to attract them. *Salvia nemorosa* 'Ostfriesland' is one I often use.

Scabiosa (scabious)

These have a lovely wild quality to them and provide lots of movement. They look great planted with grasses such as feather grass (*Stipa tenuissima*) and butterflies are sure to visit. They flower on thin branching stems and the flowers look like pretty pincushions during summer and autumn. A close relative to scabious, but just as desirable to wildlife, is the yellow scabious (*Cephalaria gigantea*), which is much taller and has a lemon-yellow flower. This looks great at the back of a border planted with taller grasses to create a wild look.

 Cut down the spent flowering stems in autumn.

Sedum (Herbstfreude Group) 'Herbstfreude' ('Autumn Joy')

'Herbstfreude' has fleshy stems and plates of tiny star-shaped flowers in pinky red, which bees and butterflies simply can't resist. It's a late bloomer and puts on its best show in early autumn, which is invaluable at a time of year when pollen and nectar supplies are starting to dwindle.

 See *Sedum*, Naturalistic Garden, page 114.

Sorbus (mountain ash, rowan)

◀ This tree is native to the UK, which makes it perfectly suited to support the UK's native wildlife. Its leaves are loved by the caterpillars of many moths, and its red berries attract some of the most stunning birds. It can grow up to 15m tall when fully mature so check your positioning. *Sorbus aucuparia* and *Sorbus* 'Joseph Rock' (pictured) are both great options.

 Remove dead, damaged or diseased growth. It will benefit from a mulch around the base, too.

Other plants for a wildlife garden

- ✤ *Berberis thunbergii* f. *atropurpurea* 'Helmond Pillar'
- ✤ *Geranium* 'Elke'
- ✤ *Geranium* 'Orion'
- ✤ *Persicaria* amplexicaulis 'Fat Domino'

Urban jungle garden

These days many of us live in cities or towns, where outside space is at a premium. Making the most of these small plots – which are often shady and awkwardly shaped – can be tricky, but it is certainly possible to create your own little peaceful oasis amidst the hustle and bustle. The key to success is to use all the space available; to do this you need to think outside the box, things that can be converted to have more than one use are especially valuable. I've written more generally about smaller spaces in the next section (see pages 132–139), but if you want to embrace the urban aspect of your surroundings and create your own 'urban jungle', this is the scheme for you.

Lush planting

Lots of evergreens and bold shapes are the basis of a successful urban garden. Large-leaved plants also work well – they create a jungle effect and give a sense of drama and mystery. For young children, it can be magical to walk under and brush up against a lush green canopy and exciting to hide among the leaves. On a more practical level, plants with large foliage are really good in urban gardens because they are better at coping with shade than smaller-leaved plants, as the large surface area of the leaf can capture more sunlight for photosynthesis.

Planting plan

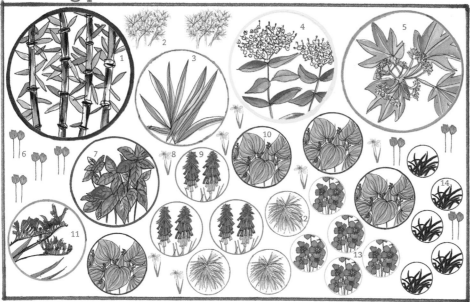

1 *Phyllostachya nigra*
2 *Foeniculum vulgare 'Purpureum'*
3 *Phormium*
4 *Sambucus Nigra*
5 *Fatsia japonica*
6 *Tulipa* – choose a bright pink
7 *Nandina*
8 *Daffodils*
9 *Kniphofia*
10 *Hosta* 'Sum and Substance'
11 *Crocosmia*
12 *Hakonechloa macra 'Aurocea'*
13 *Geum*
14 *Ophiogon planiscapus* 'Nigrescens'

Many people think that to achieve the urban jungle look you need to know a lot about tender plants, but this isn't the case. You can grow many plants that will give the look and feel of a jungle even though they aren't remotely exotic.

Large-leaved plants usually require lots of water, so adding well-rotted horse manure, homemade compost or leaf mould will help your soil retain moisture. Mulching will also help lock in moisture.

Informal shaped beds will work well in this scheme, and wide beds will give your big-leaved plants lots of room. However, if you only have a small area, don't be put off. Using one specimen architectural plant underplanted with lower-growing foliage plants can be really effective.

▲ Large architectural leaves create a great jungle effect.

Recycled objects

This style of garden is ideal for incorporating old bits and bobs in an imaginative way. Oil drums, bicycle baskets, or old stacks of painted tyres can be incorporated into the design as containers. You can also take advantage of existing features, and get creative with some subtly themed decorations, like the spider sculpture on this tree stump.

What to plant

Akebia quinata (chocolate vine)

Named for its chocolatey colour and fragrance, it has racemes of cup-shaped flowers in the spring which are a deep purplish colour. This climber is a great one to grow in a sunny, sheltered spot in the garden. It is self-twining but will need something to grow up, so tie the new stems in initially. Planting it with a paler flowering climber or against a light-coloured stone wall can give some stunning results.

 Cut back after it has flowered if it is getting too big, otherwise leave it alone and enjoy what it has to offer.

Bamboos

Bamboos are another hardy classic that is very in keeping with this style. Add extra interest by planting one with coloured stems. *Phyllostachys aurea* is one I have in my own garden and is one of the clump-forming varieties so it will stay reasonably compact.

Remove any dead canes if required, as well as leaf debris from the base of the plant. Should it get too big, you can divide in the spring.

Crocosmia

This plant has a great narrow leaf shape and sword-shaped foliage, so it looks good even before its exotic-looking flowers bloom. They flower on a branched stem, and are delicately funnel-shaped, coming in shades of bright red and orange. *Crocosmia* × *crocosmiiflora* 'George Davison' is a good choice for this scheme.

Cut the foliage back to the ground in spring.

Echinops (globe thistle)

See Family Garden, page 86.

Euphorbia

With their fabulous form of upright sparsely spaced stems and huge heads of acid green flowers, varieties such as *Euphorbia characias* subsp. *wulfenii* work brilliantly in an urban scheme, especially if planted alongside a dark-flowering *Astrantia* such as A. 'Ruby Star' for a wicked combination that will enliven any urban space.

Leave until spring, as they have attractive seedheads over winter, then remove the stems that have flowered and are now dead. Leave all the other growth alone as this will send up flowers for that year.

Fatsia japonica

This is easy to grow, likes a bit of shade and has lovely glossy evergreen leaves that are very exotic and architectural looking. When it's mature, the trunk can become a feature in its own right. It also looks fantastic when underplanted with low-growing plants such as *Hakonechloa macra* 'Aureola' to show it off.

 Remove any dead, diseased or weak foliage in the spring.

Foeniculum vulgare 'Purpureum' (bronze fennel)

▲ I love this plant – it has such a graceful quality, but the bronze foliage and bright yellow flowers give it an edge. Early in the year the foliage looks fantastic, gently frothy and adding texture. It grows up to 1.2m. If planted alongside *Verbena bonariensis*, it will give you a vibrant clash of yellow and purple in late summer, creating quite a statement in the garden.

 Leave its ghostly stems on over winter as they look incredibly pretty with a dusting of frost.

Geum (avens)

Tall, wiry stems appear from neat clumps of low foliage, giving great movement to any planting scheme. The flowers are saucer shaped and often nod in the breeze whilst mingling among their neighbours. Some varieties flower over a long period. Last year I planted *Geum* 'Lemon Drops' in my garden and it flowered from late spring to mid-autumn! I can also recommend G. 'Prinses Juliana'.

 Cut back the old stems as soon as they have finished flowering to encourage more flowers.

Hakonechloa

This looks excellent in a container or a border. It is quite low growing so good for suppressing weeds, planting around the base of trees or around the edge of a pot. There are two main varieties. *Hakonechloa macra* 'Aureola' has more golden-coloured foliage and is excellent for brightening up dark corners. The greener variety, *Hakonechloa macra*, is a stronger grower and needs more space. Both are very low maintenance. They look good from early summer right through to mid winter.

 Cut back all the foliage in spring to make way for the new growth.

Hosta

The variety of hostas to choose from is vast, but their large, lush leaves look fantastic in this style garden. If you have a small garden, ones with variegated leaves can be effective as they add more to a small space. Variegated leaves have two shades of green, or are sometimes green and white. *Hosta fortunei* 'Francee' and *H.* 'Fire and Ice' are excellent choices. Try and pick a range of sizes and heights too – this will add depth. *H.* 'Stained Glass' and *H.* 'Sum and Substance' would both work well in an urban jungle scheme.

 Slugs love hostas. Using copper tape around the pot will help to deter them, as will the wool pellets you can buy at most garden centres. Hostas take a little effort to keep free of slug damage, but are definitely worth it.

Kniphofia (red-hot poker)

The kniphofia's vibrant hot-coloured, spear-shaped flowers look fantastic when teamed with lush planting in mid–late summer. They like full sun and are best in well-drained soil, so add some grit or gravel to the planting holel. *Kniphofia* 'Primrose Upward' is a great variety.

 Old flower stems can be cut down once plants have finished flowering.

Nandina domestica (sacred bamboo)

This wonderful evergreen shrub has delicate-looking foliage and a bamboo-like habit. It gives great autumn colour and its small white flowers form on large panicles which are followed in autumn by red berries. What's not to love?

Remove any dead or damaged growth in spring.

Ophiopogon planiscapus 'Nigrescens' (black lilyturf)

This small, decorative grass is excellent for ground cover. It spreads, creating mats of black foliage that produce a bright blue flower spike. Plant alongside something with bright foliage to really bring it to life and give any garden a modern twist.

Remove any tatty or dead foliage and flowerheads in spring by cutting it back to the base.

Passiflora caerulea (blue passion flower)

You would be hard pushed to find something as exotic-looking as the passion flower, with its large blue or white flowers and intricate central filaments. It needs lots of sunshine and good support. Tying it to a trellis, fence or a warm wall will get you the best results and the most blooms from early summer to early autumn.

Fuss free. Just remove any long growth and trim if needed to control size after flowering.

Rodgersia 'Bronze Peacock'

This shrub has huge, dark, plum-coloured leaves early in the year which turn green during summer. It has a bright pink tall spray of flowers in late summer and both foliage and flower contrast brilliantly with the lush green leaves of other plants.

💧 Remove any dead foliage in autumn to prevent slugs hiding underneath over winter.

Sambucus nigra (elder)

A great shrub with wonderful dark foliage and a pink, lacy flower in summer, which can be used to make elderflower cordial or champagne. If underplanted with *Hakonechloa macra* 'Aureola', it will give you a knock-out combination of contrasting colour, form and texture.

💧 Cut back hard in spring or autumn; the more you cut it back, the more you will control its size and shape. This is essential if you are growing in a container.

Trachelospermum jasminoides (star jasmine)

A brilliant climber for small spaces – see Mediterranean garden, page 105.

Phormium

Phormiums have a fantastic form for an urban setting. With their long, sword-like leaves they look very dramatic, and come in lots of different foliage colours, from greens to reds and deep plum. Planting something of a contrasting colour and form next to a phormium will help to really show it off. Phormiums like sun and free-draining soil, which makes them good for large containers.

💧 Remove any dead or tatty foliage as and when needed.

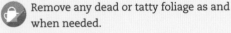

Other plants for an urban jungle garden

❀ *Nandina domestica* 'Nana' (also called 'Pygmaea')
❀ *Phyllostachys nigra*

Using houseplants

Instead of planting annuals for your summer container displays, use exotic-looking houseplants, such as arum lilies (*Zantedeschia*) and peace lilies (*Spathiphyllum*). They will all add to the atmosphere if you are creating an urban jungle. Just bring them in before the first frosts.

Small spaces

Outdoor space is a real luxury for some of us. In cities in particular, people often live in flats and have little or no access to a garden. However, some have a tiny outdoor space, such as a balcony, roof garden or basement courtyard. These can be transformed with plants, giving you pleasure and interest all year. When working within such a small space, planning and a little imagination will go a long way.

Balconies

Evergreens are a great option for a small space like a balcony as they will provide structure and colour all year. Lollipop-pruned topiary in a container looks great, and you can plant something like lavender or *Heuchera* around the base, giving you two levels of interest. Small trees can add real impact. Check the mature height and spread, but both birches (*Betula*) and *Malus* are able to grow with their roots confined to a pot. You can also buy *Malus* on a dwarf root stock, meaning they stay small and live quite happily in a container.

Using all vertical space available is the key to a successful balcony garden. The more green you can fit into a small space, the more garden you will feel you have, and using climbers will keep your floor space free.

Keep your colour choices to a minimum – I would stick with green and one other colour. Whichever two colours you choose, try and pick up on something in the property to link with the outside space.

Use all areas possible for plants. You can get some amazing containers now, which are designed to click around

▲ Plants spilling over raised beds gives the illusion of abundance.

▲ Lollipop pruned topiary looks great in a small space.

drainpipes, hang over either side of your balcony balustrade or attach to walls with ease. Lots of them also have water reservoirs built in, which is a great help. I have also seen balcony gardens with artificial turf laid as a full floor covering – this is a great way to add more green and immediately makes the space feel bigger.

Raised beds or containers also create an illusion of more space as you can see underneath them, and running a rope light or strip of LEDS under them can down-light the edges of your balcony, which looks fab in the evening – as would a string of fairy lights just about anywhere!

Front gardens

These days, most front-of-house spaces are paved or tarmacked for extra parking. This is a real shame, but it's just a sign of the times.

In wartime, front gardens were used for growing vegetables so people could feed their families, but once food was no longer rationed front gardens were reclaimed and lovingly restored to manicured plots that were very much part of the home. I would love to see some of this passion reintroduced and people taking pride in the space at the front of their properties.

The design principles are exactly the same in a front garden as a back garden. If like most front gardens your plot is smaller at the front of your house than it is at the back, keep it simple. You probably want plants that are tough and will stand up to a higher level of pollutants – and perhaps you'd like to find plants that can help with soundproofing and screening from neighbours. Using lots of evergreens will give you a core structure that will be attractive all year.

Planting plans

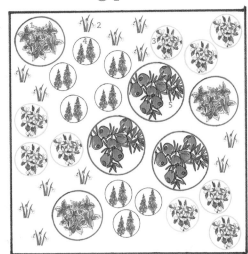

1 *Euonymus fortunei*
2 Spring bulbs of your choice – I'd recommend snowdrops to keep with the white and green scheme.
3 *Geranium macrorrhizum* 'White-Ness'
4 *Digitalis Purperea* 'Alba'
5 *Taxus baccata*

1 *Betula* 'Jackmontii'
2 *Geranium oxdnianum* 'Wargrave Pink'
3 *Sarcococca*
4 Spring bulbs of your choice
5 *Heuchera* 'Plum Pudding'
6 *Stipa teniussima*
7 *Nepeta*
8 *Euonymus* 'Green Gaiety'

Lightening the load

You have to consider weight on a balcony. Once you have filled containers with soil and plants and watered them, they will become very heavy. If weight of soil is an issue, there are artificial alternatives on the market you can mix with a multipurpose compost to give you a lighter growing medium. Perlite and vermiculite can be used, but I have found Leca to be very good.

Acer (Japanese maple)

All acers can make perfect small specimen trees. They will give you fantastic autumn colour and many have interesting bark, which is an added bonus in winter. Their delicate palmate leaves also add texture. Make sure the variety you choose will grow to the right size for the space. *Acer palmatum* 'Dissectum Garnet' is a compact variety that grows to just 1m and is ideal for small spaces. Many other varieties will stay within a 2m threshold. Acers have delicate foliage so like a bit of shelter from strong winds and dappled shade.

🪴 Remove any brown or dead stems if they appear, cutting back to a healthy bud. Only do this when the plant is dormant, at the end of autumn or before spring. A spring mulch will give it a boost.

Amelanchier lamarckii

This is a stunning small tree that can reach up to 8m at maturity – however, this can take up to 20 years. It will give you lots of rewards. It has a lovely open framework when it's mature, and the blossom it produces is a mass of very pretty white stars in early spring. Its new foliage has an attractive bronze flush and wonderful autumn colour, it also produces berries which are purpley black. It is more suited to a front garden but you could grow it in a container.

🪴 None required unless it grows too big for where you want it, in which case prune in late winter or early spring, when the tree is dormant.

What to plant

Betula utilis var. jacquemontii (Himalayan birch)

The Himalayan birch has been a favourite of garden designers and landscape architects for many years. It has striking white bark, so even if underplanted the stem is still very visible. It also has slender branches, which carry a delicate leaf. This means that in a small front garden it will not cast too heavy a shadow, just a light dappled shade, which is often desirable.

🪴 Mulch around the base of the trunk in spring.

Best bulbs for small spaces

Lots of spring-flowering bulbs take up very little room, and planting them under deciduous trees, such as an acer, means you can make the most of space in your containers. *Chionodoxa* has electric blue star-shaped flowers, *Crocus* are delicate and goblet-shaped, whilst *Iris reticulata* has stiff and narrow erect leaves and three spectacular fall petals. These are all great options. For something a little more statuesque, look at all the different varieties of *Allium*.

Camellia

These have stunning pompom-like flowers in early spring and evergreen foliage, which will give structure and a good backdrop to brighter plants in the summer months.

🪣 This plant needs acidic soil, so adding a bag of ericaceous compost to the planting hole or container if your soil is alkaline is a must for healthy growth.

Clematis 'Cezanne'

This climber reaches only 1.5m. It has large blue flowers with cream centres that bloom from early summer to early autumn. It will grow happily in a pot, just make sure to give its roots some shade by planting something else in the pot with it.

🪣 Cut back the whole plant to a few inches in spring, then either tie in the new growth to a trellis or other support, or allow it to scramble through whatever it is planted with.

Euonymus fortunei 'Silver Queen' and 'Emerald Gaiety'

If planted by a wall, these two evergreen shrubs will grow up and cover it. The great thing about them is that even though they can achieve big heights, they will tolerate being clipped and pruned to make them any size you want them to be. They are bushy shrubs with small but broad oval-shaped leaves. They are also good at providing support for more delicate plants, such as Clematis 'Cezanne' (left). They like well-drained soil and will tolerate partial shade.

🪣 Prune in spring if you need to and feed with chicken manure or seaweed. These will both be good for promoting strong, healthy foliage.

Festuca mairei

This is an arching evergreen grass that is drought tolerant. It will tolerate sun or partial shade and its foliage will stay nice and compact. Its panicles of flowers appear in midsummer.

 Easy and fuss free. Remove any tatty foliage in spring.

Dove Cottage

Geranium (cranesbill)

See Romantic Cottage Garden, page 74. *Geranium* 'Azure Rush' has medium-sized blue saucer-shaped flowers and *G.* 'Dilys' is smaller and pink. Both will grow well in the ground or in a container, so are ideal for a small garden. They will flower from early summer right through to autumn and have a relaxed, slightly sprawling habit. *G.* 'White Doves' is an evergreen variety that is excellent for ground cover, and *G. nodosum* will grow in dry shade.

Hebe

See Family Garden, page 87. *Hebe rakaiensis*, *H.* 'Pascal' and *H. pinguifolia* 'Pagei' are three great varieties for a small garden. They look good when planted in groups mingling with soft plants like *Nepeta* and *Geranium*. They will cope very happily in a container, too.

Helianthemum

A super little low-growing plant, this looks fantastic grown in gravel, where it sprawls covered in small, saucer-shaped flowers. Depending on the variety, it comes in yellow, orange, pink and white and will flower from late spring till the autumn. It will do well in a container and looks pretty when cascading down the side of the pot. It likes lots of sun and well-drained soil.

 Trim lightly after flowering if it starts to look unruly. Otherwise, leave it to do its thing.

Heuchera

I love the foliage colours of *Heuchera* varieties, but have come to the conclusion that both the peach- and green-leaved varieties are the most reliable. *Heuchera* 'Peach Flambé' looks fantastic all year, as does *H.* 'Marmalade'. The purple-leaved ones like *H.* 'Plum Pudding' look great in containers too. However, I would treat them as an annual, as they seem to exhaust themselves in the first year and never really recover.

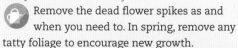 **Remove the dead flower spikes as and when you need to. In spring, remove any tatty foliage to encourage new growth.**

Hosta

Mainly grown for their foliage, these are fantastic plants for containers, if only because it's easier to keep the slugs away. Planting the ones with the most interesting foliage colour will bring depth and further interest to your small space. I like using *Hosta* 'Sum and Substance' in pots as it is large-leaved and architectural, although small varieties like *H*. 'Patriot', with its white margins, are good in small containers. Hostas will tolerate shade, which can be very useful in a town garden.

 Cut back the dead leaves in autumn and mulch around the crown in the spring.

Other plants for small spaces

- ❀ *Digitalis purpurea f. albiflora*
- ❀ *Euonymus fortunei* 'Harlequin'
- ❀ *Geranium macrorrhizum* 'White-Ness'
- ❀ *Geranium × oxonianum* 'Wargrave Pink'
- ❀ *Nepeta × faassenii* 'Junior Walker'
- ❀ *Stipa tenuissima*
- ❀ *Taxus baccata*

Nepeta racemosa 'Walker's Low'

This is a fantastic plant that is great for ground cover. It produces clouds of blue flowers for months if given enough sun and well-drained soil.

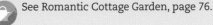 See Romantic Cottage Garden, page 76.

Sarcococca (Christmas box)

This evergreen shrub has the most stunning smelling flowers. They are tiny white stars, which hang under the leaf joint in the depths of winter. A good plant for adding structure to any space, it likes partial shade.

Leave alone unless it starts to get too big for its space, then prune in spring after flowering.

Stipa (feather grass)

See Family Garden, page 90.

Rental properties

If you're renting, you might feel apprehension at the thought of putting down your roots and getting stuck into a garden that isn't yours. Usually it is stated in most rental property contracts that it is the occupier's responsibility to maintain the current garden. In reality most people do the bare minimum, as they don't see the investment in their time or money as being worthwhile. However, we also want to be able to enjoy the space and make the most of it, so what is the best way around this?

Container gardening

I tend to advise most people in rental properties towards containers, as you can take these with you when you move house. There is a huge range of plants that will grow happily in pots, from small trees and formal topiary to herbs and shallow-rooted vegetables, such as lettuces or radishes. As long as the pot is large enough to accommodate the plant and you keep watering, the plants will grow happily.

The basic design rules are the same whether you're planting in the ground or in a container – you can create tiers with the different heights of pots and plants. You can plant one specimen in a pot and make it a focal point.

Containers can be a feature in their own right – you can buy them in all kinds of different colours and shapes, or even transform them into water features. Using fairy lights and garden lanterns will also enhance the garden. Regardless of your rented garden space, you can make it your own with a bit of imagination – the beauty being that the whole lot can be transported when you move.

▶ *Miscanthus nepalensis* at Dove Cottage.

Dove Cottage

Chapter 4

Planting, care and propagation

Now that you have learnt about your garden,
worked on your design, and chosen your plants, it's time to get
down to the real business of creating your new borders and
gardening. This chapter will guide you through preparing your
borders, planting, caring for your plants to make sure you get
the most from them, and propagation.

Preparing the borders and planting

In order to achieve healthy, successful borders, you need to make sure that you prepare properly first. Here's how to create a border from scratch, and how to make sure it's ready for the plants.

Creating the borders

Once you have drawn up the plan of your garden (see page 38) and worked out where you want your new borders to go, you'll need to mark out the area. You can use string and canes to do this, or spray paint – even a hosepipe laid on the ground would work. If you have any paving or flags that need lifting, make sure all the foundations are removed; old concrete, builders' sand and rubble will prevent your new plants from getting their best start.

If you're lifting a lawn or area of grass you could hire a turf-lifting machine, but they can be heavy and awkward. Instead, you can do this by hand. I find the easiest way to do it is to divide the area with a lawn edger into sections of approximately 30 x 30cm. Then, using the blade of your spade horizontally, lift and remove the sections just below the grass roots, usually 5–8cm deep. You can pile these turf sections on top of each other green side down and cover the heap in something that will exclude the light, yet allow it to breathe, like weed membrane. After a year, you will have a lovely fibrous loam to use on the garden or in your containers.

Digging and improving soil

To give your plants the best start, dig over the soil to at least a spade's depth – this is particularly important if the area has not been used for planting before. This will help break up hard clumps and any compacted ground that new roots might struggle to get through and will improve drainage. Removing any large stones and perennial weeds at this point is also essential (see page 148).

Once you have roughly dug your bed you can begin to dig in some bulky organic matter, such as homemade compost, well-rotted horse manure or leaf mould (see page 147). This will benefit all soil types by increasing fertility, improving drainage and helping water retention. If you have clay soil, it's a good idea to add some washed river sand (available online if your local garden centre doesn't stock it) or horticultural grit to help improve drainage.

Ideally, it's best to prepare the ground a few weeks (at least) before you want to plant. Turn the soil over every now and then and remove any weeds you might have missed.

'No dig' method

If you're not in a hurry to plant your bed you could try the 'no dig' method. Instead of digging over the bed, which can be hard work depending on the size, you can smother your bed in a thick layer of organic matter (homemade compost, well-rotted horse manure or leaf mould); I would suggest a depth of at least 15cm. Autumn would be the best time to do this. Over the next few months, the worms will come up and drag the nutrients down into the soil and the frost will break up the clods of earth. By spring, the ground should be much more workable and ready for planting.

▶ I find a small border fork useful for getting in and amongst the borders.

Planting

When planting, read the label and make sure you are allowing enough room for the plant to grow. Trees and shrubs will obviously take much longer to get to their mature size, but perennials and annuals will, in most cases, get to the height and spread on the label within the first year or two. Dig a hole about 20cm wider and deeper than the pot the plant is still in. You can add some manure, leaf mould or compost to the hole to give the plant a head start and, if planting trees and shrubs, a sprinkling of fertiliser can be beneficial. However, if you regularly mulch your garden, your soil should be good enough to skip this step. Place your plant in its new planting hole and back fill, breaking down any clods of soil into small crumbs as you do so. The plant wants to be in the soil to the same level it was in the pot. Firm down around the plant to make sure there are no air pockets and give your plant a big drink. If planting a bulb, just remember that all bulbs like to be buried to at least two and a half times the depth of the bulb. For sowing seeds, see pages 156–157.

Planting containers

Make sure you have drainage holes in the bottom of the container and before planting place crocks or gravel in the bottom of the pot so excess water can drain away.

Using a good multipurpose compost is fine for all plants, but if you have any leaf mould or homemade compost to add to the mix, all the better.

Caring for plants

To keep your garden in tip-top condition you must be prepared to put in some time on maintenance. Nature is never static: something is always changing and not always for the best. So to keep your garden growing in the way you envisaged will take a little work.

Watering

Water is the life force of any plant. Just like humans, plants need water in order to be able to grow, survive and procreate. It is essential that plants be given the water they need in order for them to be able to thrive.

The first job after planting is watering, to give them a drink and settle the roots into the soil. Thereafter you need to water new borders and containers regularly. In the height of summer I would water a new border at least three times a week – you will be able to tell when it needs it just by looking at your soil to see if it is dry and at your plants to see if they show signs of wilting. As your garden matures you can water less, as the plants will have a sufficiently strong root system to go in search of their own supply. Containers are different – it is essential that you keep watering them regularly. In summer I water mine every day (unless it has rained) for the best displays, as plants in pots do not have the capacity to go searching for water themselves – they rely solely on you and the rain. It is important to never let the soil in your containers dry out.

How to water

A hose can make watering borders a much easier task, and the money spent on having an outdoor tap fitted will save you hours of toing and froing with the watering can. I would suggest you measure your garden and make sure that the hose you buy will reach exactly where you need it to – having to join two together every time you want to water can be a real pain. It may be that two outdoor taps fitted at different points works best, or you use a hose for the back garden and a water butt for the front. Water butts are a must in any garden, no matter how small; collecting rainwater is a simple and cost-effective way to make sure your plants get what they need.

It's best to water plants in the evening, after the sun has gone down. Water can evaporate quickly at midday, and having excess water on the leaves when the sun is at its strongest can result in leaf scorch. The roots are where we want the water to go, and the deeper the water penetrates, all the better for the plants, as this will encourage the roots to extend deep into the soil, resulting in a much sturdier, tougher specimen. I tend to aim the hose at the base of the plant and count ten 'Mississippis' before I move on to the next plant.

▼ **Always water at the roots, not the flowers themselves.**

Feeding

When it comes to feeding plants in my own garden as well as my clients', the only thing I do is mulch in the spring. If done thickly, this is all that is needed.

You can look out for signs of nutrient deficiency in your plants, which will show in their leaves – they usually start turning yellow. But before you start feeding them, consider other factors, like poor drainage, bad weather or pests and diseases. It is rare that a plant suffers from nutrient-poor soil. Some plants can be particularly hungry though, such as *Buxus* and roses, so you can give them an extra feed in early summer with pelleted chicken manure. Your containers will need feeding regularly as they only have what you give them. I use tomato feed, as it has a high potassium content which is good for encouraging more flowers, fruit and vegetables. Just follow the instructions.

Liquid feeds

There is a wealth of liquid feeds on the market, should you need them. Seaweed feeds are popular. They provide potassium, magnesium and trace elements, and are a more organic and sustainable option. However, you can also make your own liquid feeds with very little effort. Comfrey is a very attractive plant that you can grow in your borders or vegetable plot. Take a bunch of torn-up comfrey leaves and place them in a bucket with water to the point that it just

covers them. Leave them in a dark place for a couple of weeks and ta-da! Now your brew will not only smell potent, it is also extremely concentrated, so dilute with three parts water.

Chicken manure

You can buy this in tubs from the garden centre relatively cheaply. Just sprinkle it over your borders in early spring to give them a boost. It's super easy and quick to apply. It's high in nitrogen, which promotes healthy foliage. If you keep your own chickens, the manure will need to be stored in a heap until it is well rotted and no longer smells of ammonia before applying to any plants.

Mulching

Mulching is the process of applying organic matter to borders. It feeds plants, improves the structure of the soil and is a brilliant way of suppressing weeds. The best time to mulch is in spring, ideally after a good downpour of rain to lock in moisture. If you mulch at the beginning of the season you'll find your borders get a head start, freeing you up to do other jobs in the garden.

Once you have cut back your borders and the soil around your plants is exposed, spread a thick layer of mulch over the surface of the soil around your plants and everywhere in between. There are many different types of mulches (see below). The worms will come and take down the nutrients

from the mulch right to the roots of your plants.

Alternatively, you can use a weed-suppressing membrane and then cover it in mulch (see page 149). Personally, I prefer using mulches on their own; they look more natural and the plants can grow uninhibited, stretching their legs and self-seeding. A weed-suppressing membrane prevents this from happening as the seed that drops will not come into contact with the soil.

Homemade compost

This is wonderful stuff, and completely free! Find a corner of your garden and either build a compost bin out of old pallets or buy a plastic one. The advantages of non-plastic types is that there is more opportunity for air to be able to get to the compost, and this helps to speed up decomposition. You can cover your heap with old carpet or a sheet of weed membrane, but it isn't essential. A plastic bin will always come with a lid.

You can compost vegetable peelings, eggshells, shredded paper, plants that you have cut back in the garden – but not weeds! Lawn clippings and thin cardboard which you have torn up can also go in. Even items that are either 100% wool or cotton can go in. The key to successful compost is a balanced mix of ingredients: usually 70% vegetation versus 30% carbon-rich materials (paper, etc.) works the best.

Do not attempt to compost meat, or anything cooked. Shiny, laminated paper is also a no-no, but at the top of the BANNED list is WEEDS.

Keep adding to your heap, and every now and again stick a garden fork in and jiggle it around to let air in. Pour a watering can full of water over it every month or so to speed up the process a little. Don't be too generous, though; you want moist, not wet, compost.

Within 6–8 months you should have a medium that resembles soil – black and crumbly with a lovely sweet smell (well I think it smells sweet, or maybe that's just the sweet smell of success!).

Leaf mould

Another garden freebie! Collect up all your leaves in autumn (see box below) and put them into a black bin liner. Sprinkle in a little water, expel all the air out of the bag, then seal it tightly. Using a garden fork, prod through the bin liner to make lots of air holes, then put the bags out of sight somewhere – under a hedge or behind a garage – a stack of bin liners isn't the prettiest focal point! Every month or so, give the bags a shake. After 12 months the leaves will have broken down and the leaf mould will be ready to use on your borders.

Horse manure

Well-rotted horse manure is a fantastic soil conditioner and plant feed. If you live near stables, ask the owner if you can take some manure – they are usually glad to see the back of it. However, remember it is safe to use on the garden only once it has completely rotted down. Take it from the bottom of the heap – it should look like black crumbly soil; if it still looks and smells like fresh manure, don't use it as it could scorch the foliage of your plants. If you can't collect it from a farm or stable, you can buy it in bags from most garden centres.

Mushroom compost

You can buy this by the tonne from many local topsoil suppliers. It's a great feed for the garden and is usually pretty cheap. However, it can contain large amounts of chalk, which will increase the alkalinity of the soil. Use it on acidic soils that are low on organic matter, but don't use it on soils that are already chalky or alkaline.

Collecting leaves

This is a tip from the great gardener Geoff Hamilton. Sweep all your leaves into a long, thin pile, then mow over them with your lawn mower. Not only does this save your back from all the bending over to collect them, it also chops the leaves up into smaller bits, which speeds up decomposition, giving you wonderful leaf mould to use on the garden far quicker than if you left them whole.

Weeding

Every garden contains weeds.
They have adapted to survive
and are extremely successful
plants. So successful, in fact,
that if left to their own devices
they would take over our
gardens, making it impossible to
grow cultivated varieties of the
plants we love. They take
nutrients and water from the
soil, and block out the sunlight,
making it hard for other plants
to compete. If only everything
we planted was as floriferous
as weeds!

Most people see weeding as
backbreaking work, and it
certainly can be if you take on
an overgrown plot full of
invasive weeds. The first time
you dig over the area and
attempt to get rid of all the
roots it will be a big job – but it's
essential to do it, particularly
for the more pernicious weeds
such as horsetail, ground elder
and bindweed (see pages
150–151). However, once you've
done this and applied a mulch,
regular hoeing for the rest of the
season should keep most of the
weed seedlings at bay.

Hoeing

Use your hoe to slice through the top-growth of the seedling, cutting it off just below the surface. Doing this means the top-growth will shrivel and die and the root will not be able to photosynthesise. This won't work with all weeds – those with deep taproots, such as dock and dandelion (see page 151), will grow back from the tiniest segment of root left in the earth and you will eventually have to take your daisy grubber to them, but regularly hoeing their top-growth will certainly weaken the plants. Using a hoe on your border will also disturb any weed seeds that are just starting to germinate.

Hoeing is also great for those who don't have much time to maintain their garden; you can wiggle and shimmy through a border very efficiently and at great speed with a hoe, and whether you remove the top-growth of the weeds you have sliced or leave it on your border is up to you. I remove it and hoe my footprints out. The finished look should be a weed-free border with a lovely open texture of soil. It's very satisfying and will instantly make your garden look smarter.

If you can manage to hoe once a week from early spring to late summer – great! (If not, once a fortnight would also allow you to just about keep on top of things.)

Using weedkiller

Some people opt for off-the-shelf weedkillers. These can be effective, but it is important to follow the instructions carefully. It's best to use weedkiller on a still, dry day, to reduce the risk of killing something you don't want to. Most weedkillers these days are systemic, which means you spray or paint them onto the leaves of the weed and the poison travels down to the roots where it kills the plant. Many people think using weedkiller will save time and effort. However, you have to remove all the debris the weedkiller has created so you might as well just remove them by hand in the first place. I also think that mulching and working the soil has an overall healthier effect on the garden.

Weed-suppressing membrane

Also called geotextile membrane, landscaping fabric or sheet mulch, a weed-suppressing membrane is a lightweight UV-stabilised fabric that allows water through but reduces or blocks light and so prevents weed germination and growth.

Weed-suppressing membrane has several uses. Where the soil has not been cultivated and is overrun with weeds the fabric can be laid over the whole bed – the lack of light will kill off the weed's top-growth, making the bed easier to dig. If planting a new border you can cover the prepared area and make holes in the fabric to plant through. In an established border you can cut the fabric to fit around existing plants. You can cover it with composted bark or gravel, depending on what would be most in keeping with your scheme.

Types of weed

Weeds are particularly difficult to identify at the start of spring, before the flowers appear. Here is my list of the most common weeds and the best ways to eradicate them.

Ground elder (*Aegiopodium podagraria*)

A perennial thug, this plant grows via networks of roots just under the surface of the soil. It has a distinctive lobed leaf and flat heads of cream flowers. It grows to around 45cm (18in). Loosen the soil and try to remove as much of the white web of roots as you can by carefully using a garden fork. It is extremely persistent and once it has taken hold it can be very difficult to eradicate completely from the area.

Bindweed (*Calystegia sepium, Convolvulus arvensis*)

▼ As the name suggests, this is a strong climber that will wrap around anything it can, causing congestion and choking plants. It has heart-shaped green leaves and a trumpet-shaped white flower. The roots are thin, long and white, branching out to cover large areas. Loosening the ground with a fork and gently pulling the roots out is the best option. It can be very satisfying when you manage to get an extra long bit! Another form of control is to place tall garden canes where it grows. Once it has grown up the canes you can remove it without damaging any plants it would have grown up and through.

Hairy bittercress (*Cardamine hirsuta*)

With their small rosettes of green leaves, these can look innocent at first, but don't be fooled. If left to go to seed, this plant can explode its load with astonishing force! Pull them out as soon as you see them, which is easy as they have very little in the way of roots. If you allow them to develop flowers and seeds, you won't see the back of them for years.

Common chickweed (*Stellaria media*)

Forming dense mats of small green leaves with tiny white flowers, this plant can grow from a single seed and produce flowers and seeds of its own within 5–6 weeks, meaning potentially thousands more seeds spreading throughout your borders. They are relatively easy to pull out by hand. However, if you find this difficult use a garden fork to loosen the soil around them – this will free up the roots and make them easier to get out.

Horsetail (*Equisetum arvense*)

This weed looks Jurassic: small brown cones full of spores poke through the soil in spring, then the rest of the plant grows like small fir trees invading. It has a thick, waxy stem, and is difficult to eradicate even with the strongest weedkillers. Damaging the leaves will help absorption of a glyphosate-based product, if that's the route you want to take, but you'll have to reapply it several times. A more organic approach is to keep hoeing off the tops of the plant and covering the ground with thick weed-suppressing membrane to block out any light. Over time, this should weaken and exhaust the plant. Be prepared for the long haul with this weed – it's not to be underestimated.

Creeping buttercup (*Ranunculus repens*)

This is my nemesis. I hate the stuff! The leaves are similar to a few varieties of geranium, which can make it tricky to identify. However, it manages to take over borders by sending out stolons like a strawberry plant. These are long, thin stems that come from the base of the parent plant. Once a few inches long, they touch the ground and another bloomin' buttercup grows! Act quickly, or before you know it you will have an army of them to deal with marching through your beds. Even though the roots are shallow, they are extremely fibrous and will hang on for dear life when you try to pull them out. It's best to use your fork and dig them out fully, shaking any excess soil back into the bed.

Bramble (*Rubus fruticosus*)

◀ Boisterous and thorny, this is a tough weed to tackle. If you can manage to cut it back to where it is growing from, that's great. However, brambles root-tip just like the stolon on the creeping buttercup. Wherever they touch the ground a root will form and another stem will leap into action, giving you a tangled mass. Starting by digging out with a garden fork wherever it has root-tipped and following it backwards is your best bet. It can be painstaking, but the hard work now will ease the work later on. Try to wear long sleeves and thick gloves; brambles can be vicious.

Groundsel (*Senecio vulgaris*)

This flowers from early to mid-spring, has a height of around 45cm and a small yellow flower. Groundsel is very toxic to animals, so remove it immediately if you have pets or livestock. It can spread quickly but pulls out easily, so is one of the more manageable weeds.

Dandelion (*Taraxacum officinale*)

Last but by no means least, this has large, dark green, deeply cut leaves, distinctive yellow flowers and an enormous fleshy taproot resembling a small cream carrot. This weed easily grows back from a tiny section of root left in the ground, so you'll need to dig out the whole root using a trowel or daisy grubber.

Beneficial weeds

Some weeds, such as stinging nettles (*Urtica dioica, U. urens*) and broad-leaf dock (*Rumex obtusifolius*), deserve a place in your garden. They provide early food for ladybirds, seeds for birds and many moth and butterfly larvae will feed on them. If it's a wildlife garden you want, a small patch is certainly worthwhile. I would never suggest allowing these to grow in your borders next to your prize dahlias, but they could be tucked away in a hidden corner, alongside the compost bin.

Keep the nettle in check by cutting it down in autumn and digging out areas where it is spreading beyond where you want it. Dead-heading the docks once they have flowered will prevent them from dropping seed. If you want to remove dock completely, dig down deep – they have taproots that can reach a staggering 5m underground!

Supporting plants

Some plants will need to be staked in your borders, depending on what you have planted, especially when the plant is young and has yet to bulk up. It can be a fiddly and fussy job if left until the final hour – you end up with a plant that loses its natural form and looks all trussed up and regimental. To avoid this, get your supports in nice and early. I do them in early spring, when the plant has got enough new growth that you can make out the width of its crown.

I have tried many techniques over the years, but have found that this one works the best on perennials. You can buy small plastic trellis (ideally green) on a roll from most garden centres. It usually comes in two different widths – 1 foot or 1 metre. I cut a length so it measures approximately 12–13cm bigger than the circumference of my plant, then – using canes to weave through the plastic and hold it in place – I create what can only be described as a 'girdle'. The plant will grow through the support, disguising it while it spreads to create a natural shape.

If you need to stake a tree, first make sure your stake is substantial enough to support your tree. Then hammer the stake into the ground at a 45 degree angle to the tree trunk and secure with a rubber tree tie in a figure of eight. This will create a cushion between the stake and the tree, protecting the bark from any possible damage caused by rubbing against the stake.

Dead-heading

Dead-heading regularly and feeding is a must to keep your containers looking tip-top. Dead-heading from early summer is best – once you move into autumn, I tend to leave the flowers to set seed to provide winter structure and food for the birds. Dead-heading is simple. Using a pair of secateurs, simply snip the flowerhead off all the way back to a new leaf joint.

▲ Dead-heading is an important part of plant maintenance and keeps everything looking great.

Dividing plants

Sometimes herbaceous plants have done so well that they are growing into other plants. Where this is the case, you can control them by division. This is also a useful way to propagate plants, as if planted elsewhere in the garden or in a pot the removed plantlets will form new plants (for more on propagation, see pages 156–161). Perennials that have been in for several years can sometimes go woody in the centre of their crown with new growth coming up around the edges. When this happens, it's good to dig up and divide the plant, removing the woody stuff that's not growing and replanting the newest clumps of shoots. This will be really beneficial to the plant, giving it much more vigour.

How to divide perennials
This should be done in late autumn or early spring. Cut the foliage and dead flower stems down to the ground so you can see the crown of the plant and water well. Using a fork, dig under the root ball and prise it out of the ground. Once it's out, the standard method is to use two forks back to back to divide the root ball where it divides naturally to give you smaller pieces, each with some roots. Many people are concerned about breaking roots and being too rough, but I have divided perennials by slicing through them with a spade and breadknife before, or using my hands.

When you have divided your plant, take the new divisions and plant them elsewhere in the garden, or pot them up and give them to other gardeners. Add some organic matter to your new planting hole – this can be homemade compost, well-rotted horse manure or multipurpose compost. Replant and water well.

▲ Astrantias can be propagated by division.

▲ If you divide at the correct time of year, very little can go wrong.

Cutting back plants

Many people prefer to cut back at the end of the season, which is late autumn to early winter. This is fine if you prefer to work that way. Just one thing to be aware of, though – if you live in an area which is susceptible to cold winters, leaving on the dead top growth of your perennials can help protect the crown of the plant.

The 'Chelsea chop'

This is a really useful method of stunting the growth of a plant so the flowers won't flop under their own weight later in the season. It is also a way of delaying flowering. The procedure takes its name from the Chelsea Flower Show, as it needs to be carried out around the time of the show, in late spring. It involves cutting back two-thirds of the plant's growth using a pair of hedge shears or secateurs in order to promote shorter, stockier stems and bushier growth.

Examples of plants that benefit from the 'Chelsea chop' include Sedum (Herbstfreude Group) 'Herbstfreude' ('Autumn Joy') and S. *spectabile* cultivars. By the time these plants bloom at the end of summer the flowers are often so heavy that they cause the plant to collapse and reveal its rather bald-looking crown – not very attractive. However, if you give them the 'Chelsea chop' you can avoid this, as the stems will be shorter. It is also useful to delay the flowering time of some plants. For example, if you have two

clumps of *Helenium*, cut back the one closest to the front of the border so when the clump behind has finished flowering the one in front will take over, extending the season of interest.

Pruning

Pruning can differ from plant to plant, and is usually dependent on when the plant flowers. Pruning is done not only to restrict size and create healthy shaped plants free from congestion, but also to help with fruit and flower production as well as encouraging new growth. For example, training fruit trees to grow horizontally against a wall by pruning them in a certain way will give you heavier crops of fruit. The tools required for the job are secateurs, lopers and pruning saws – these are all straightforward and easy to use.

A little saying an old college tutor told me still swims around my head when I am pruning. It goes: 'Remove dead, diseased, damaged, weak and crossing wood'. You should always do this for any tree or shrub, whatever the species, as leaving the wrong shoots on the plant can have detrimental effects. Dead shoots serve no purpose, diseases can spread, damaged shoots can leave the plant vulnerable to infection and weak shoots take valuable nutrients that the rest of the plant would benefit from. 'Crossing wood' means branches or stems that rub against each other, sometimes creating an open wound that exposes the plant to attack by harmful pests and diseases.

How to prune

The position of a pruning cut is very important, as it affects how well the cut will heal.

1 Always make a cut to a bud or leaf joint – any part of the shoot left above a bud or leaf joint will die back and turn brown, leaving the plant vulnerable to pests and diseases.

2 Wherever possible, cut a stem on the diagonal (at a roughly 45 degree angle), sloping downwards from the bud or leaf joint. This encourages rainwater to drain off rather than sitting on the wound, where it will inhibit the healing process and can cause the stem to rot.

3 It's best to prune to a bud or new shoot that faces outwards from the plant, as this will provide a good open framework and help air to circulate around the plant. It also prevents stems from crossing.

Winter protection

Some plants in your garden may need winter protection. One of the best ways to protect vulnerable plants is horticultural fleece. You can either cover the plants with it and pin it to the ground or wrap it around a plant. In most cases it is the crown of the plant you're trying to protect. If you have something with large leaves like a

Dicksonia tree fern, folding the plant's dead leaves onto the crown and then wrapping it in fleece will help give added protection. Some plants, such as *Gunnera*, will be happy with just their leaves folded onto the crown. If you are growing tree ferns, they may also need straw or fleece packing into the crown before you proceed to wrap them in fleece, depending on the severity of winters you have.

Pests and diseases

Another thing that can cause you plant problems is pests and diseases, of which there are too many to list! My advice is to keep a list of plants you have. That way, if you see any bugs on your plants and the plants begin to look sick (to show any type of leaf deficiency, mould, discolouration, wilting, holes, etc.) you can do a quick internet search using the name of your plant and find out what pests and diseases it is susceptible to. I always look at treating things as organically as possible first, before I resort to chemicals.

Propagating plants

Propagating is essentially getting lots more plants for free. It is usually really straightforward and takes little time, making it incredibly rewarding. But don't put the pressure on – it doesn't always work, even for the most experienced gardener. Have a go and always try to propagate more plants than you think you will need, spreading the chances of success. Remember, drainage, moisture and light are three basic requirements of all propagation techniques.

▲ Cardoon seed heads make a great architectural winter feature.

▶ These purple *Verbena bonariensis* struggle to survive outdoors in a cold winter, so I collect their seed each year to make sure I can grow them again.

Sowing seed

The most basic form of propagation is sowing seed. For the vast majority of plants you will want to grow it is incredibly straightforward. You can either collect seeds from a perennial or annual and store them in an airtight container until you want to use them, or buy packets of seed from a garden centre, nursery or mail-order company.

Collecting seed

It's so satisfying to collect seed from your own plants and increase your stock for free. Although not all plants will grow successfully from seed, many

will do (see page 161 – propagation list). Where I live the winters are hard and cold and some of my favourites, such as *Verbena bonariensis* and *Cerinthe major*, won't survive outdoors, so collecting their seed every year is an easy and cost-effective way of making sure I always have plenty in my garden. There are some plants like *Anemone nemorosa*, *Ranunculus* and *Primula japonica* which should be collected when they are unripe and green.

Leave the seedheads on the plants until they are brown, as they need to dry out. It is best to collect seeds from plants in the evening after a sunny, dry day. Keep an eye on the plants you want to collect from – if you miss your window, the seed pods will have opened and dropped their seeds. All you need to do to collect the seeds is snip the flowerheads off and shake them upside down into an envelope or paper bag. Remember to label them so you know which is which! They will keep well in their paper packets inside an airtight container until it is time to sow them.

If you are sowing herbaceous perennial seeds or seed from annuals, it is best to sow in early spring, as the warmer temperatures will aid with germination. If you have a greenhouse or cold frame, you can sow in autumn.

How to sow seed

Most seed is sown in early spring, when it will generally germinate with ease, but if you're buying seed always follow the instructions on the packet as times and methods may vary. There are various methods for sowing seeds, from indoors in pots or trays to sowing in situ outside.

Sowing in pots and trays

Annuals, perennials and vegetables are all suitable for growing in pots or trays.Create a shallow drill, space seeds down the drill 5cm apart and cover with soil. Adding vermiculite to your compost before sowing will add lots of air pockets for the new fragile roots to get through.

Stand the pots or tray in a larger tray without holes and pour some water into the tray. The water will seep up through the compost. Watering this way (rather than the surface of the compost) means that the seeds won't be disturbed from their positions. Keep the soil moist at all times. Some seeds will benefit from extra heat, but it will tell you this on the packet. If you have collected the seed from your garden and are unsure, consult the internet.

Pricking out and potting on

Pricking out is when you lift some of the seedlings and replant them into individual containers so they have more room to grow.

Plants are ready to prick out once the seedlings have developed a pair of leaves. To prick out, gently take a leaf between your forefinger and thumb and, using an old lollipop stick, carefully ease the roots out of the soil. Plant the seedling into a larger pot and water as often as needed – never allow the soil to dry out completely. You may have to prick out once more if the seedlings start to compete for space in their pot. Always label your plants so you know what you've grown.

Give your seedlings lots of light, but avoid direct sunlight. Protect the seedlings from any late frost that will damage or even kill them.

Once your seedlings have begun to bush out, and have several sets of leaves and roots that touch the bottom of their container, they are ready to go outside. If you have sown annuals in a greenhouse you will need to harden them off. This means putting them outside on a frost-free day at the start of spring and taking them back under cover in the evening for a few days. Once the risk of frost has passed, they can be planted out. It is a good idea to harden off perennials too, but once planted out the frost won't kill them. Plant them in the same way you would plant anything else (see page 144).

Sowing direct into the ground

Make shallow drills in the soil 3–4cm deep using the tip of a trowel or a garden cane. Then sow seeds into the drill, leaving 10cm between each seed. Cover with soil and water, making sure you have a rose on your watering can. You want to sprinkle water lightly, not slosh it, disturbing your seeds.

will just be able to fit more in!) You can use multipurpose compost for this, and mix in a bit of your homemade compost if you have it. Adding vermiculite or grit to your compost will help the delicate roots to form. Insert your cutting so two thirds of it is submerged. You can easily get six cuttings in a 1-litre pot. Water well.

4 Cover the pot with an old clear shower cap and place in a warm, bright place, but out of direct sunlight. The shower cap helps keep them warm and moist while letting light in.

5 Once roots have established, which can take a couple of weeks, pot each cutting in its own pot and leave until the plant is large enough to plant out in the garden.

Division
See page 153.

Taking cuttings
Taking cuttings is a really easy method of propagation once you have had a few goes. All you need is a pair of sharp secateurs to do the job and it takes minutes. It causes no harm to the plant you take material from and is also a great way to save money and get lots more of your favourite plants.

Softwood cuttings
Softwood cuttings are taken from plants in early summer while the shoots are still soft and pliable and before the tissue has turned woody. Lots of herbaceous perennials and some shrubs can be propagated in this way.

1 Take a cutting from the tip of a healthy new shoot around 10cm (4in) long.

2 At the bottom of the cutting, cut straight across directly underneath a leaf joint and strip the lower leaves from the stem. Using your fingertips, pinch out the growing-tip; this will encourage the cutting to bush out.

3 Fill a 1-litre pot, if you have one, with compost. (Any bigger than this is also fine, you

Basal cuttings

These are almost the same as softwood cuttings, except they are taken from the new growth at the bottom of herbaceous plants. Choose sturdy new shoots and use a knife to cut the stem away from the base of the plant, including part of the woody tough bit just under the new growth. Then treat in exactly the same way as a softwood cutting.

Hardwood cuttings

Hardwood cuttings are usually taken in autumn, but you can also take them in winter. They are really straightforward and a good way to propagate shrubs.

1 Choose a stem to take your cutting from. It needs to be the current year's growth and should be as thick as a pencil and 15cm long.

2 Cut straight across below a leaf joint, then on the diagonal above a leaf joint.

3 Push the base of your cutting into a pot that is deeper than your cutting. Space around the edge of the pot, leaving a gap of 5–10cm between each cutting. Use multi-purpose compost mixed with some homemade compost for this. Leave 2.5cm of the cutting showing above the soil. Water well and place outdoors in a frost-free, sunny place over winter.

4 Once roots have developed in spring, replant into individual pots until they become established and large enough to go in the garden. You will know when they are ready when you see a few new shoots appearing and the roots have reached the bottom of the pot.

Semi-ripe cuttings

Climbers, shrubs, herbs, and trees can all be propagated in this way. Semi-ripe cuttings should be taken from this season's growth, so the base of the cutting should be hard and the tip soft. The best time to do this is early summer to mid-autumn. Once you have cut your material from the plant you need to get it into compost as quickly as possible.

1 Prepare your cutting by cutting it to around 15cm. As with a softwood cutting, cut straight across at the bottom below a leaf joint. Strip the bottom leaves from the cutting and trim the remaining ones by half to prevent water loss.

2 You can then dip the bottom of the cutting into rooting hormone powder, which is available at almost all garden centres. If you don't have any, you may well have success without it.

3 Insert the cuttings into a suitably sized pot, which has been filled with a 50/50 mix of potting compost and either perlite or vermiculite.

4 Gently water and cover with a plastic bag. I find a disposable shower cap works well. Place in a light position out of direct sunlight and don't allow the soil to dry out completely.

Root cuttings

These are to be taken from herbaceous perennials in late autumn or early winter. Plants with thick fleshy roots work best, such as oriental poppies, *Acanthus*, *Phlox*, *Echinops* and *Verbascum*.

1 Unearth a section of the plant you want to take cuttings from, and choose some long roots that are of finger thickness. Cut them off and cover your plant back up with soil.

2 Get rid of the thin root end and cut the rest into sections of around 5cm. Cut straight across at the top and at a 45 degree angle at the bottom so you remember which way your cutting needs to be potted.

3 Fill suitably sized pots with a 50/50 mix of potting compost and either grit or perlite and push your cuttings into the mix so the horizontal cut is just below the surface. Then cover the soil and cuttings with a 1cm layer of grit.

4 In the spring, you should see new shoots and your cuttings should have their own root system. Pot them on individually until they look sizable enough to plant out.

Layering

This is a nifty little bit of propagation that is good for shrubs and climbers.

1 Take a long, flexible shoot that will bend down to the ground. Give the stem a nick on the underside on a clear section of stem between two buds.

2 Pin the stem to the ground using a tent peg or piece of bent wire. Make sure the open wound comes into contact with the ground, as this is where the new roots will develop. You can water it a little if needed.

3 If you have been successful, new growth will sprout after a few weeks and it will develop its own root system. Once it has done this, you can detach the new shoot from the parent plant. Dig up the new plant and move it to the spot where you want it to grow on.

Clever or what?

Garden surprises

Plants can cross-pollinate in the garden to give weird and wonderful variations of certain seeds and their characteristics. For instance, if you collect and sow seed from an *Echinacea* plant there is no guarantee that your new seedling will have the same colour, vigour and health as the parent. This is because the plant may have cross-pollinated with another Echinacea, resulting in a genetic variation and creating something new. This is what makes growing from seed particularly exciting, and plant breeders cross-pollinate plants all the time in order to take the best characteristics from two plants to create an even better variety.

If you want an *Echinacea* identical to the parent plant the only way to propagate is by division (see page 153). The piece of root with a shoot you take off will grow up to be an exact replica of its parent plant.

Propagation methods

Acer **softwood cutting/ seed**

Achillea **division/seed**

Agapanthus **division**

Agastache **division/seed/ semi-ripe cutting**

Akebia quinata **seed/ layering**

Alchemilla mollis **division /seed**

Allium **seed**

Amelanchier lamarckii **seed/semi-ripe cutting**

Anthemis **division/seed**

Aquilegia vulgaris **seed**

Aruncus 'Horatio' **division/seed**

Aster **division**

Astrantia **division**

Bamboo **divison**

Berberis thunbergii **semi-ripe cutting**

Betulis utilis var. jacquemontii **grafting/ seed/softwood cutting**

Buddleja **softwood cutting**

Buxus sempervirens **softwood cutting**

Calamagrostis brachytricha **division**

Calamintha **division**

Camellia **semi ripe cutting**

Ceanothus **semi-ripe cutting**

Chamaerops humilis **seed**

Choisya ternata **semi-ripe cutting**

Cirsium rivulare 'Atropurpureum' **seed/ division**

Clematis **layering/seed**

Cotinus coggygria 'Royal Purple' **semi-ripe cutting**

Crambe cordifolia **seed/ root cutting**

Crataegus laevigata 'Paul's Scarlet' **hardwood cutting**

Crocosmia **division**

Crocus **seed**

Cupressus sempervirens **semi-ripe cutting**

Delphinium **basal cutting**

Digitalis **seed**

Dipsacus fullonum **seed**

Echinacea **division/seed**

Echinops **division/root cutting**

Erica carnea **semi-ripe cutting**

Erigeron annuus **seed/root cutting**

Euonymus **semi-ripe cutting**

Eupatorium **division**

Euphorbia **basal cutting/ division**

Fargesia **division**

Fatsia japonica **semi-ripe cutting**

Festuca mairei **division**

Foeniculum vulgare 'Purpureum' **seed**

Galanthus **division/seed**

Geranium **division**

Geum **seed/division**

Hakonechloa **division**

Hebe **softwood cutting**

Helenium **division**

Helianthemum **softwood cutting**

Helianthus annuus **seed**

Heuchera **division**

Hosta **division**

Hyacinthoides non-scripta **seed**

Ilex crenata **semi-ripe/ seed/cutting**

Kniphofia **division**

Lavandula **semi-ripe cutting**

Lilium **offsets** (this is another word for division of bulbs – you take the small new bulbs that have developed around the parent bulb and re-pot on their own)

Lonicera nitidia **semi-ripe cutting**

Lonicera japonica **layering/ softwood cutting/ semi-ripe cutting**

Lupinus **seed/basal cutting**

Lythrum **division**

Malus sylvestris **seed/ grafting**

Molinia **seed/division**

Monarda **division/basal**

Nandina **semi-ripe cutting/seed**

Narcissus **offsets**

Nepeta **division/ softwood**

Nerine bowdenii **offsets**

Olea **semi-ripe cutting/ seed**

Ophiopogon **division**

Origanum **division/seed**

Passiflora caerulea **seed/ semi-ripe cutting/ layering**

Pelargonium **softwood cutting**

Perovskia **softwood cutting/semi-ripe cutting**

Persicaria affinis 'Superba' **division**

Persicaria amplexicaulis **division**

Phlomis tuberosa **division/ seed**

Phormium **seed/division**

Phyllostachys **division**

Pimpinella major 'Rosea' **seed/division**

Potentilla fruticosa **softwood cutting**

Rodgersia **division**

Rosa **hardwood cutting**

Rosmarinus officinalis **semi-ripe cutting**

Rudbeckia fulgida var. Sullivantii 'goldsturm' **division**

Salvia **division/semi-ripe cutting**

Sambucus nigra **softwood cutting/ hardwood cutting**

Sanguisorba **division/ seed**

Sarcococca **semi-ripe cutting/ seed**

Scabiosa **seed/division**

Sedum **division/softwood cutting**

Solanum crispum 'Glasnevin' **semi-ripe cutting**

Sorbus **hardwood cutting**

Stachys byzantina **division**

Stipa **division/seed**

Thalictrum **division**

Thuja occidentalis **semi-ripe cutting**

Thymus vulgaris **seed/ basal cutting**

Trachelospermum jasminoides **layering/ semi-ripe cutting**

Trachycarpus fortunei **seed**

Tulipa **offsets**

Verbascum **seed/ division/root cuttings**

Veronicastrum **division**

Chapter 5

Beyond the borders

Although the main focus of this book has been your beds and borders, you need to think about the rest of your garden too. From lawns to decking and lighting to water features, there are plenty of extra ways to give your garden sparkle.

On the ground

One of the main considerations, given that it's often what most of the space in the garden is made up of, is your ground covering. Getting the balance and materials right here will help show off your magnificent new borders.

Lawns

If you have a tiny urban garden you most likely won't have the space for a lawn. However, in the majority of larger gardens, especially those that need to provide an area for children to play, a lawn will be a key part of the design. Like a rug in a living room, the lawn becomes a void that will give balance to the mass around it (in the case of a garden – your borders).

Like all plants, the grass that makes up a lawn needs looking after. To keep a lawn looking good it requires mowing once a week in spring and summer and in some parts of the country it will also need a regular trim over winter, as it never really stops growing. It will also need feeding and weeding in spring and autumn, as well as scarifying, in the spring. To scarify, pull a leaf rake through your lawn vigorously. This will help pull out any moss and dead grass, allowing air to circulate and new grass shoots to emerge. You will need to pay particular attention when dealing with problem spots such as under dry trees or shady damp areas, as grass will never really thrive in these situations. So the positioning of a lawn within the garden is key to how successful it will be.

◄ **Keep your edges neat! It can smarten up your whole garden in an instant.**

Artificial lawn

Many of my clients are put off gardening as they don't feel they have enough time to maintain a lawn. Five years ago I would never have considered using an artificial lawn in any of my designs. However, in recent years artificial lawns have come on in leaps and bounds and can be so good that you are hard pushed to see the difference.

I would recommend spending as much as you can afford on artificial grass; also, have it installed by a professional, as it makes a difference to the finished look. If artificial turf is going to enable you to spend more time enjoying your garden, it really is worth trying.

Decking

Decking is also a viable option for levelling an area which is uneven, sloping or prone to waterlogging. Any level changes in a garden are good as they add lots of interest and the opportunity for a seating area.

I like to use green oak as it weathers really well, but you can now choose from an enormous range of wood stains so can paint or stain it in any colour you like. Composite decking is made from recycled plastic and is also another fantastic option. It can be so good that even the professionals find it hard to tell the difference between composite decking and real wood. If you are a dab at

◀ Here, a raised area of decking including a summer house adds an element of magic to a naturalistic garden.

smooth and hard. Not only is it attractive, it sets incredibly quickly and is porous, so will drain well.

Paving

The range of paving on the market is huge. It's a good option for paths and patios and, unless in full shade, where it can sometimes get covered in moss and algae, it will take little maintenance. The paving you choose can give a very different feel to your garden, so consider your theme and surroundings when choosing. If you intend to be in your property a long time, buy the best stuff you can afford. It will last much longer and age better.

DIY then decking is pretty straightforward, however if you have any doubts, go and get the professionals in.

Gravel

You can get gravel in different sizes and colours. If you already have gravel in the garden, try and match the new colour with the old. If you are starting from scratch, look at the colour of the brickwork on buildings around you and use similar coloured gravel for a harmonious link to the surrounding area. Gravel is a good weed suppressant, yet allows things to self-seed freely. It is also often used as a security measure as you can't walk quietly on gravel.

Resin-bound gravel is wonderful stuff. It makes stunning sleek walkways, patios and driveways in a wide variety of different colours. It's essentially very small gravel set into resin, so it isn't loose, but

▲ Choose materials to complement your planting.

Gabions

Gabions are large wire mesh cages that can be used for retaining banks on sloped areas. They are really strong and are usually filled with stones or cobbles, but they can be filled with anything that fits your garden theme, like glass bottles, house bricks and pinecones. Many plants, particularly alpines will grow out of pockets of soil within them if you want to soften the look. Just fill sections of the gabion with soil, mixing in a bit of homemade compost if you have it. Then push your alpines through the wire mesh squares, tucking them into the soil. You may have to divide the plants to make them small enough to go through the holes. This is a job for autumn or early spring.

Boundaries, screens and dividers

Whether you want to create a bit of privacy, screen a less attractive part of your garden (such as a bin store or shed), or simply divide your garden into different areas to create 'rooms', there are lots of ways you can incorporate dividers into your garden design.

Fences

Fences make a great backdrop for plants and give you vertical space to grow climbers. They can be painted to enhance and tie in with your planting schemes and, depending on what style of fence you choose, can add either a traditional or a more contemporary look. Some fences have trellis incorporated in the top section. A more natural looking fence could be woven from branches of hazel, whilst for a modern look you can use long batons of cedar horizontally, leaving a shadow gap between each baton. This gives you clean linear lines to plant against.

Walls

Low walls are good at dividing the garden and double up as seating. Walling can be used to create terraces and raised beds. Seek professional advice if you want to build a tall wall, as this may need planning permission. And consider your materials – tying your walling material to match that of your property is a good option if you are not confident enough to know what else might look good with your design.

▲ Fences make a great backdrop for plants.

Living walls

Also known as green walls, these are the garden rock stars at the moment. All the coolest and newest buildings have them, and trendy architects are having them installed inside and outside their latest creations. When done well they look incredibly beautiful and make a real impact, even in the smallest of spaces. The trick is to grow a mixture of mostly low-growing plants that will offer colour and cover all year.

Most living-wall installations are done by specialist companies and come with their own watering system that can be set on a timer. The company will plant it for you with a variety of plants they know to be suitable for the site. If you're feeling adventurous, have a go yourself – you can buy the walls separately and grow what you like on them. Strawberries do very well as the slugs can't get to them up high and they're at the perfect height for picking.

Hedges

Hedges give a softer boundary edge than walls or fences and are great at filtering wind. They are also incredibly beneficial to wildlife, giving them shelter, food and nest materials. However, depending on what plants you use, hedging can require quite a lot of maintenance.

The plants you choose for hedging can create very different aesthetic effects in the garden. A native wildlife hedge gives a naturalistic look and is perfect for a garden within a rural setting, while box (*Buxus sempervirens*) can be clipped and trimmed to any shape you like and will give a more formal feel. Bamboo provides great movement and a gentle sound as it sways in the breeze. It works brilliantly if the right varieties are used – if not, it can be a real thug. *Fargesia nitidia*, *Phyllostachys flexuosa* and *Pseudosasa japonica* are all well-behaved options.

▲ Colourful foliage adds interest to your garden.
▶ Clever planting can be used to create more subtle boundaries within your garden.

▲ Hedging, like this yew hedge, can be used to divide your garden into areas.

Water and
water features

Water adds great atmosphere to a garden. Whether it's a still pond, a fountain or a contemporary water feature, they all bring a garden to life.

Ponds

Still ponds instill a sense of calm – they reflect the sky and aid contemplation. They are also invaluable to the local wildlife, which will gravitate towards any expanse of water, no matter how small. How you want to incorporate a pond into your garden design will dictate how it should be planted up, if at all.

Wildlife pond

A wildlife pond needs an array of plants to be sustainable. Deep-water aquatics, which sit on the bottom of the pond, are essential for oxygenating the water and preventing the growth of algae. Marginal plants, which are planted around the edges on shelves within the pond, provide shelter for wildlife as well as helping with access in and out of the pond. Water lilies (*Nymphaea*), water hawthorn (*Aponogeton distachyos*) and surface plants, which float on the

surface and don't need soil to grow, will provide cover and shade – ideally at least one third of the water should be shaded. As with garden plants, many pond plants can be invasive and clog up a pond. It's vital that you read the label and try to use as many native pond plants as possible.

Modern water features

Modern water features come in all shapes and sizes, from fountains in ponds, to cascades using natural stone or free standing urns that fill with water which then trickles down the side of the pot into a water reservoir below. You can buy them off the shelf at most garden centres or create your own with a little imagination. They are also great for giving vertical interest, and add lovely sound and lots of splashy fun for children. Metal grids can be installed in many ponds and water features just below the surface of the water to protect children's safety. You will need an outside electricity supply to be fitted by a professional.

▲ Big, lush leaves overhanging a pond or water feature will give your garden a natural look.

Pond maintenance

Keeping your pond in good condition is essential. Remove dead plant debris regularly. You may also get blanket weed, which looks like floating mats of green algae and resembles hair when lifted out. It can choke plants and effect your pond life, so remove as soon as possible. See an aquatic specialist at your garden centre if the problem persists. In late summer, before the leaves begin to fall, cover your pond with a fine net. Fallen leaves release gases that cause the water to stagnate and can have a detrimental effect on wildlife.

Outdoor lighting

In the last few years I have designed more and more gardens with outdoor lighting incorporated into them. From a practical point of view it makes the garden more useable and for longer periods of time and, as a designer, I love the different looks and moods you can create in a garden using light and interesting shadows. For example, an uplit tree can add a sense of drama and become a fantastic focal point; a water feature with submersible spotlights can be extremely atmospheric; a pathway or series of steps simply lit can create a sense of mystery and excitement; and fairy lights wrapped around a pergola or coiled around the trunk and branches of a tree create a magical feel to any garden. Do not underestimate the draw of fairy lights – they are definitely not just for Christmas!

There are many forms of lighting that operate using solar panels – the adventurous among you might even opt for coloured lights. Any more ambitious lighting installations should, of course, be fitted by professionals.

White plants

If you spend a lot of time in your garden after dark, consider planting plenty of white plants. At night white plants really stand out and, if coupled with lighting, they will transform your garden, creating an entirely different feel from the daytime.

Resources

Books

***The Complete Planting Design Course* by Hilary Thomas**

This was on the syllabus for my university course and is a great resource for garden design.

***A New Perspective* by Piet Oudolf**

A great book to look at for jaw-dropping visuals – sure to get you inspired.

RHS Plants for Places

A valuable guide for what will grow where.

Online

National Gardens Scheme (NGS)

All the garden featured in the NGS Yellow Book and on its website are great places to visit for inspiration and free advice – plus it's a great charity!
www.ngs.org.uk

Royal Horticultural Society (RHS)

A great place to turn to for sound knowledge and advice.
www.rhs.org.uk

Pinterest

If you're looking for inspiration, Pinterest is a great place to start. You can look at thousands of images and create your own pinboards to pull ideas together.
www.uk.pinterest.com

Gardens in this book

A special thank you to the owners and keepers of these gardens, who allowed us to visit their sites to take photographs for this book.

Burton Agnes Hall & Gardens, North Humberside
www.burtonagnes.com

Capel Manor, Enfield
www.capelmanorgardens.co.uk

Cow Close Cottage, North Yorkshire

Dove Cottage, Shibden, Yorkshire
www.dovecottagenursery.co.uk

Hillbark, Bardsley, Leeds
www.hillbark.co.uk

Jean Hall and Jean Holdgate, Eldwick, Yorkshire

Jungle Garden, Leeds

Scampston Hall, Malton, Yorkshire
www.scampston.co.uk

York Gate, Adel, West Yorkshire

Yorke House, Nidderdale, North Yorkshire

Index

Acknowledgements

Thanks to everyone at Kyle books for taking a punt on a Leeds lass with terrible spelling and to my editor, Tara, for making the process pretty chilled and not half as terrifying as I expected.

A huge thanks to all the gardens from the NGS scheme for letting me photograph their stunning gardens (full list on page 170). Keep up the great work, guys. And a very special thanks to Kim and Steven at Dove Cottage in Shibden for always being a massive source of inspiration.

My gardening mentor Jean Hall, I hope my passion for gardening is still as fierce when I have been doing it as long as you have. You rock.

Paul Debois, I thoroughly enjoyed time spent with you shooting gardens, thank you for the great pictures. Dale and Polly, you made the whole thing so pretty, yet practical! Thanks so much.

To my fiancé Ed for just being generally amazing and incredibly supportive. I can't believe I actually get to marry you. My daughter Polly for always being positive and great fun, the force is strong in you, don't forget it. I love you both endlessly.

And lastly I'd like to pat myself on the back. I never thought I could or would ever write a book and I have. Well done me.